HOLDING GOD
HOSTAGE

HOLDING GOD
HOSTAGE

TOM WATSON, JR.
& STAN SCHMIDT

Wolgemuth & Hyatt, Publishers, Inc.
Brentwood, Tennessee

The mission of Wolgemuth & Hyatt, Publishers, Inc. is to publish and distribute books that lead individuals toward:

- A personal faith in the one true God: Father, Son, and Holy Spirit;

- A lifestyle of practical discipleship; and

- A worldview that is consistent with the historic, Christian faith.

Moreover, the Company endeavors to accomplish this mission at a reasonable profit and in a manner which glorifies God and serves His Kingdom.

Unless otherwise noted, all Scripture quotations are from the Holy Bible, New International Version. © 1973, 1978, 1984 International Bible Society. Used by permission of Zondervan Bible Publishers.

Wolgemuth & Hyatt, Publishers, Inc.
1749 Mallory Lane, Suite 110
Brentwood, Tennessee 37027

Library of Congress Cataloging-in-Publication Data

Watson, Tom, 1918–
    Holding God hostage / Tom Watson
and Stan Schmidt.—1st ed.
        p.   cm.
    Includes bibliographical references and index.
    ISBN 1-56121-044-7
    1. Schmidt, Stan, 1954—Mental health. 2. Manic-depressive psychoses—Patients—United States—Biography. 3. Manic-depressive psychoses—Patients—United States—Religious life.
I. Schmidt, Stan, 1954– . II. Title.
RC516.W35 1991
616.89′5′0092—dc20
    [B]   90-23745
                                                                        CIP

Secreting themselves in closets of shame—
across this nation and presumably around
the world—are multiplied thousands
of unhappy people whose chemical
imbalance has laid upon them the stigma
of "mental illness." Other earnest folk vainly
seek escape from debilitating mood swings—
and other physical afflictions as well—
through demands of faith based
upon presumption rather than
God's specific promises.

To all of these,
with fervent prayer
for their deliverence through trust,
understanding, and acceptance
of a sovereign God's better way,
this book is lovingly dedicated.

TOM WATSON, JR.
STAN SCHMIDT

CONTENTS

Introduction / 1

1. Facing the Consequences / 5
   Handling a Serious Illness / The Death of a Son / Challenging Their Faith / Misguided Theology / Depression: Number One Illness

2. Out of the Padded Cell / 29
   Melancholia: Friend or Foe? / Diagnosis of Depression / The Faith-Healing Question / Safeguards

3. A Disintegrating World / 57
   Struggles of the Caregivers / Ancient Cures / Modern Approach / Testing Faith with Snakes and Cyanide / Defining Presumption / Reckless Deeds for God? / Man's Desire for Power and Control

4. Who Needs This Messiah? / 85
   Reclassifying the Disease / Postponing the End / Use of Lithium / Watchtower Society / Accepting the Risk

5. Changes for the Better / 107
   Deliverance from Demons: The Debate Continues / Enter Presumptuous Faith / Christian Science: Manslaughter?

6. On Guard Against Presumption / 135
   A New Freedom / Elements of Faith / Beware the False Prophets / Fraudulent Information Sources

7. The Roller Coaster Ride / *163*
   More Letters Come / Help Near at Hand

8. Exit the Happy Ending / *179*
   *Frank's Story / Validity of Faith Healing / Twisting God's Arm /
   Oral Roberts's Tragic Life / Confidence in God*

Appendix A:
Suggested Resources on Depression / *195*

Appendix B:
Suggested Readings on Presumptuous Faith / *199*

Index / *201*

About the Authors / *205*

INTRODUCTION

This book is about a great deal more than Stan Schmidt's painful struggles with a bipolar dysfunction. That odyssey might hold interest for many, but I would be skeptical about its enduring importance.

The reason I provide this introduction is my profound concern for thousands—dare I say millions?—of people who may someday walk where Stan has walked. Too frequently I must counsel patients at risk from the same danger: an ever-so-sincere but nonetheless presumptuous faith which disregards medical reality in favor of the notion that they are a divine exception to the rule. The risk springs from their confusion about the relationship between their biological dysfunction and their personal faith in a God who is loving and merciful.

I speak as a scientist, not as a theologian, but I reason that when I exercise faith, the outcome does not depend upon my spiritual qualifications—how fervently I believe or how insistently I voice my petition. Rather, it depends upon the *truth* and *reality* of what I believe. Truth and reality, I must conclude, exist quite independent of what I'd *like* them to be. My personal challenge is to make sure what I believe is really true and truly real.

As a practitioner of the art and science of medicine, my credentials might be questioned when I express my views on the subject of presumptuous faith. I am not a theological authority. Besides, Stan Schmidt is my patient, and it's been my duty and privilege to stand by him during the ups and downs of his mood swings. Thus it may be difficult for me to speak objectively concerning the book Stan and author Tom Watson, Jr., have produced. Still, I feel compelled to join my voice with theirs.

When Stan discontinued his prescribed medication, he acted in courageous response to a challenge from those who wanted him to have what they thought was best. But in interfering with Stan's medical regimen they acted in gross—perhaps even culpable—ignorance of scientific evidence. When I learned my patient had responded to their challenge by discontinuing daily doses of lithium carbonate, assuming he or his friends had some special influence with God, I shook my head in disbelief.

These well-meaning teachers assured him it is not the will of God for His people to suffer affliction. That simplistic rationale for healing ignores mountains of compelling evidence to the contrary. Some nevertheless conclude that dependence upon doctors and medicines is evidence of insufficient faith. Stan's teachers urged him to demonstrate his newfound confidence in God, accept his deliverance, expect a miracle, and claim a life free from the inconvenience, embarrassment, and expense of doctors and medicines. As one dedicated to healing human ills I wish with all my heart wellness could come that easily!

Stan was confident his healing would happen precisely as his spiritual advisers promised him.

"Stan, trust God for a miracle if you want to," I pleaded with him, "but for heaven's sake take your medicine until you're sure the miracle has happened!" Perhaps that philosophy is akin to Ronald Reagan's famous "Trust, but verify"—words he used when he spoke of disarmament treaties with the Russians.

I see no reason why verifying cannot go hand in hand with trusting. Stan, however, saw my counsel as a message of doubt, not of faith. His friends had conditioned him not to think in such negative terms. He overlooked the fact that God also provides the miracle of medicines and healing skills.

Much time has passed since all that took place. Stan is still a man of considerable faith, but I consider him wiser and better informed. By any standard he is healthier, mentally and physically. His painful but convincing learning experience provides the underlying reality for this book. Today more than ever—and I wish to discourage no act of genuine, informed faith—I stand by my prescription: "Take your medicine until it happens." At the time those words came spontaneously out of a deep concern for my patient's health, but they may also be words of practical wisdom for others in a similar dilemma.

Physicians may be just as qualified as theologians to testify that *merely believing something does not make it true.* Stan had not thought that through, and the mistake cost him dearly. His misled and presumptuous faith teaches us that *when our premise is not true it makes no difference how sincerely or how loudly we believe it.* No matter how enthusiastically or insistently we express our faith, an untrue premise remains just that—still untrue.

In my opinion, belief in God and the desire to do His will are based upon indisputable evidence that He is there, that He is good, and that He offers a happier eternity and a preferable way of life to those who come in faith. I am grateful that Stan's commendable faith survived his ordeal unscathed. He goes on believing, with considerably healthier premises for his faith.

Presuming upon our Creator for a very personal and intervening miracle serving only the comfort or convenience of ourselves does not seem to me a reflection of Biblically oriented faith. Go ahead and believe it if you like, but I advise you to *take your medicine* until the miracle comes!

FRANK BOLEA, M.D.
Diplomate, American Board of Psychiatry
and Neurology

1

FACING THE CONSEQUENCES

Y ou should sit down, Stan." Through the telephone by my hospital bed came the voice of my Jewish mother. I had admitted myself—one sick Christian!—into a psychiatric ward. That fact may seem incongruous, seeing that this was faith healer Oral Roberts's medical center in Tulsa, Oklahoma.

"Mom, I'm *lying* down—in a hospital," I replied. "Did someone else die?" Several months before, my life had been shattered by my father's untimely death from injuries suffered in an automobile accident.

"Nobody else died." It was my mother's *don't be a dumbbell* tone. "Someone called you on the telephone. I'm telling you about it now—so you shouldn't be standing."

"I'm *not* standing, Mom. I'm lying down in a bed. So who called me?" I insisted.

"A man from California, asking for you. How could I tell him my son is in a *psychiatric* ward?"

"What man? Tell me, Mom." My impatience was the remnant of a lengthy hyperactive mood swing.

"He's from that magazine—the one you sent stuff on your . . . uh, healing."

"You mean, *Voice* called me?" Before the relapse I would have rejoiced. Now the news was disturbing. Three months before, I had written to the magazine's editors, offering to tell the world about my miraculous faith healing. I billed myself as a *former* manic-depressive. After the magazine's lengthy silence I had despaired of getting a response. Now, since I had crashed and fallen again into the depressive phase, I didn't *want* a response.

"That's the magazine about Jesus and faith healing, right?" she prodded. "Well, the man wanted to talk to you because you wrote him about being healed."

"Oh, good Lord, Mom!" What followed is best described as a stunned silence.

"Hello? Stan, are you listening?"

"Yeah, Mom, I'm listening." I was also wondering if there were a way to hang myself with the telephone cord.

"The man said they'd definitely like to publish your story about deliverance from manic-depression. You hear that, son? It's going to be in the magazine. So what will you do now? They want to tell everybody you're *healed*, that you don't need your medicine anymore."

"I'm *not* healed, Mom. You know that." I got the words out in spite of what seemed a crushing weight parked on my chest. "Yeah, some of my friends said I was healed—claimed it for me in faith—so I threw away my lithium." Then I choked on the words: "But I crashed, Mom. I didn't get healed. I'm still a bipolar . . . guess I always will be."

"So what will you tell the man from the magazine?" was my mother's insistent reply. "He said you should call him back. He wants you to hurry."

"Okay, Mom. Yeah, I'll do that." A firing squad would have been a welcome alternative. "Just give me his number and I'll call him back—but I can't do it right now."

"He said you should hurry, Stan. He said there's a deadline."

"I know, Mom, a deadline. I . . . I'm glad you called." After I got the number and said good-bye I felt tired and alone. In the name of Jesus, friends had rebuked the demons they said caused my disease and commanded them to go away. I praised God louder than any of them. Sure, I told them *I had the faith* to claim deliverance, and I proved it with a flourish by flushing my lithium carbonate pills down the toilet. Was that what is meant by *presumptuous* faith? The futility of it all caused me to sob like a baby.

My room on the thirtieth floor offered a panoramic view of Tulsa, but little was visible due to the early winter storm which had gripped the state since the previous day. Slowly placing the receiver back in its cradle, I dragged myself to the window and stared through my tears into a curtain of gloom. A wet combination of sleet and snow shrouded what seemed more than ever a bleak and unfriendly world.

How do you handle it when your faith has failed you? What do you do when you announce to the world the miracle of your healing and deliverance, then discover from a bed in a psychiatric ward the humiliating truth that nothing has really changed? Faith's claims were made in all sincerity and my prayers seemed Biblically correct. As surely as I've ever believed anything I believed God for my deliverance. Christian friends could testify to my no-turningback commitment to miraculous healing. But without my medicine I was painfully aware that manic-depression still had the power to make this zealous, bornagain Christian an emotional basket case.

꿳   꿳   꿳

Handling a Serious Illness

America's number one illness these days is depression—the "common cold" of psychiatric medicine. The dysfunction is by no means confined to people deficient in faith. Distinctions of religious views or spiritual maturity have little to do with the onset of this devastating affliction, which doctors now view as a physical, not a mental, disorder. The problem lies in the body's chemistry, as it does with gout, diabetes, and other imbalance disorders.

"More than twenty million Americans will suffer an episode of depression or mania during their lifetimes," writes Demitri F. Papolos, M.D., Assistant Professor of Psychiatry at the Albert Einstein College of Medicine in New York. His book, *Overcoming Depression* (New York: Harper & Row, 1987), classifies the disorder as psychiatrists now consider it: a chemical imbalance, not a form of insanity. Dr. Papolos's book offers emotionally troubled Americans—the chronically depressed and the manic-depressive as well—an escape from the stigma of what historically has been mistakenly referred to as a *mental illness*. Words like *crazy, demented, insane,* or *sick* are seldom appropriate for people in the throes of depression.

Like *Overcoming Depression,* this book provides a way for unwilling riders on the emotional roller coaster of mood swings to emerge from their closet of shame and reckon with the bright and controllable side of their affliction. Hiding the agonies of depression or denying its unfortunate reality leads to loss, not gain. This book will speak soberly but charitably of yet another human frailty from which too many of us suffer needlessly—the instinctive recoiling from adversity. We can handle anything but affliction!

Presumption or Faith?

Too often we mold God to our own design, naming and claiming what *we* want instead of recognizing the transcending importance and rightness of what *He* wants. How few of us submit in faith to His perfect will, *really believing* He loves us and provides unerringly what is best!

Stan Schmidt's nearly fatal mistake was assuming God was obliged to heal him. Because he "had the faith" to believe, he was confident his healing would happen, but his motive was ego-centered and his faith proved presumptuous. He gave priority to his desires; he placed emphasis upon *his* faith instead of upon the sovereign will of God. Stan was convinced renouncing his medicine would validate God's power and prove to the world the greatness of his faith. His doctor urged him *not* to take that reckless step. "Believe God for a miracle if you want to," the psychiatrist counseled him, "but for heaven's sake take your medicine until it happens!"

Stan's story also explores special problems which may escalate when faith is presumptuously applied.

Naively credulous, this fledgling believer accepted the challenge given by his teachers. At their instigation he rejected medical help and claimed his faith deliverance from manic-depression. Unaware of abundant scriptural evidence to the contrary, he believed a disease-free body was guaranteed him as a by-product of his faith in Christ. Urged on by well-intentioned teachers, at the time his trusted friends, Stan threw away his lithium pills. But in spite of determined faith and an almost childish expectancy, his mood swings returned with a vengeance. Thus Stan has personal reasons for warning others against impulsive acts of presumptuous faith. His experiences speak to Christians of all persuasions, however sincere their convictions and regardless of the nature of their fervent petitions to a sovereign God.

Encouraging Christ's Body

Stan's experience with manic-depression and the results of his presumptuous claims of deliverance are recounted here not to discourage but to encourage people of genuine faith. These experiences will speak directly to many who are mystified by their mood swings or frustrated by other recurring physical symptoms. Some Christians have been badgered into believing these adversities make theirs a second-class spiritual citizenship. Whatever your circumstances, remember that God "knows His sheep by name" (see John 10:11) and acts unfailingly in those sheep's best interest. Whether you experience a miraculous healing or are left with your "thorn in the flesh" (see 2 Corinthians 12:7–10), this book is intended to help you move from the shadow of an imaginary stigma and assume your rightful role in the always victorious kingdom of heaven.

For victims of depression, and their codependents as well, this book can provide enlightenment and a fresh start by bringing a clearer understanding of the physical or chemical dysfunction often responsible for these disturbing symptoms. Such afflictions do not distinguish between those who profess faith in Christ and those who remain unconvinced.

When any of us are struck by emotional disturbance, the relevant questions to ask are not "What's the matter—don't I believe God?" and "Am I being punished for some sin?" but "What physical or emotional problems are my heritage?" and "What is the chemistry of my blood?" The personal agonies of depression are now known to often be the consequence of biochemical imbalance. In many cases that imbalance is genetically acquired and is usually correctable.

Now, at last, victims of this potentially destructive affliction, armed with the truth, can seek informed diagnosis and counsel, and can actively participate in an effective treatment plan. Best of all, they can go right on living useful and effective lives.

The Death of a Son

Stan is not alone in his act of presumption. Larry and Lucky Parker of Loma Linda, California, working with author Don Tanner, wrote the book *We Let Our Son Die* (Eugene, OR: Harvest House, 1980), a step-by-step account of how their misguided doctrines claimed the life of their eleven-year-old diabetic son, Wesley. The Parkers' tragic ordeal of misguided faith, based more upon their imaginations than upon a specific divine promise, began when an evangelist preaching at their church took Wesley by the shoulders and prayed for his healing.

Earlier, his invitation had been broad. "Anyone who needs a miracle in their life—especially healing of the body, maybe an emotional healing, something to do with financial matters, relationships, anything you would like to have prayer for—please come," he pleaded.

All his life Wes's father had been taught the importance of exercising faith and lots of it. He was convinced if people would believe God enough to ignore the external circumstances, then their faith would be complete and they would have control, not the circumstances. If he'd ever needed control, surely this was the time—control over the ability of Wes's body to manufacture insulin. Larry believed that it was all a matter of fervent faith and confident prayer.

Deep Waters of Faith

During Larry's brief Bible college experience, a chapel speaker had exhorted the students, "You must swim out until there's no ground under you, no support at all, except the buoyance of that deep water of faith. Let Christ lift you up. . . . Float in your faith to God. . . . Strike out for that deep faith." Challenges like that are not easily forgotten.

Well, now is the time to put it all together, Larry thought as he lay awake the night after the evangelist prayed for Wes's healing. For Wes's sake he would "float in his faith." Larry determined to claim his son's healing and swim toward the deep until his feet could no longer touch bottom.

The next morning, doubts forced their way in again. Wesley's routine urine test was positive. With disappointment etched on his face, the boy held his insulin-filled syringe and motioned his father to give him his shot.

"No! It's a lie from Satan!" Larry said impulsively, grabbing the syringe from Wes's hand. Then he held his son by his shoulders and looked into his eyes. "Wes, we're not going to believe that test, okay?" He squirted the insulin into the trash and broke the needle. "You're healed—remember?"

Wesley's eyes opened wide and a smile crept across his darkened face, bursting finally into a broad grin. His childish mind had been waiting for that word of encouragement. He had given his heart to Jesus, but he was no theologian. He must depend upon his parents to interpret God and help him understand what was meant by all those complicated things in the Bible. Now his trusted interpreter had spoken, and on the authority of his father's assurance he could believe he was no longer a diabetic.

Challenging Their Faith

That night Wes wet his bed—a sign his body was starved for insulin. Was that just another satanic lie to challenge his parents' faith? In the morning Lucky fought her unbelief by taking all of Wesley's medicine from the refrigerator and tossing it into the trash can. The parents must prove to God—and, indeed, to themselves—the greatness of their faith. To be sure the medicine was out of temptation's reach, Larry took it to the city dump.

When he returned, Wesley's stomach was hurting badly and he complained of a headache. Larry's faith faltered momentarily. "I need to go to the drugstore to get some more insulin," he told Lucky. "Wesley's worse and I'm scared."

"No, we have the victory about his healing," she said. "We need more people to pray, that's all." Soon five of her friends gathered in the bedroom. And how those women prayed! "Heal Wes, dear Jesus. Let the manifestation of Your healing appear even now. We command these symptoms to go and Satan to loose his hold on this boy, in Jesus' name. Jesus, let Your healing mercies flow upon Wesley." It was all done in power, with the proper terminology, and according to the formulas.

"My head hurts. Could you be quiet?" It was Wes's muffled voice as he moaned and turned his face toward the wall.

At four the next morning Larry called his pastor, apologized for the early hour, and asked him to come at once. Wes seemed barely conscious.

Wrestling with Demons

The pastor joined the prayer vigil while Larry wrestled with the demons he felt must be preventing the healing they had claimed. "In the name of Jesus, you leave!" he commanded the devil himself. When Wesley showed slight improvement the prayer warriors held a praise meeting. "He's healed—praise God, he's healed!" Larry shouted. "A demon was in his pancreas, feeding on his insulin, but it's gone. The battle's over and we've won the victory!"

If it was a victory, it was short-lived. Wesley's condition worsened again. Friends came and prayed, exorcising demons, reciting Bible verses, and commanding the boy's healing. In the afternoon a frightened pastor returned with a sobering message for the parents. "Take Wesley to the hospital," he advised. "I think he needs a doctor."

"Taking him now would only demonstrate doubt," Larry protested. Doubt could emasculate the power they were calling down. By this time the boy was gasping for every breath.

Lucky thought of the way Jesus delayed His coming to Lazarus in John 11 so He could raise His friend from the dead. Weeping, she asked, "Could it be that God wants us willing to let Wesley die so that he can be resurrected?" Somehow they must prove to God they really did have faith.

Death Comes Quietly

That afternoon, as three praying friends sat opposite them in the small bedroom, the grieving parents held Wes's hands and continued their vigil. Suddenly, the boy's labored breathing ceased.

"Wesley's with Jesus now," Larry said, as if in a trance, "but he'll be coming back." Now they knew! Resurrection was what God had in mind all along. Nothing could shake them from that conviction—not even the police, who appeared shortly and began asking questions.

"I don't think we'll need a funeral," Larry told a surprised undertaker. "A casket won't be necessary because our son's not going to be buried. Announce it as a resurrection service," he added.

The event was scheduled for Sunday afternoon at two o'clock. Not surprisingly, reporters and TV cameramen were there when the Parkers arrived for the service.

The ceremony got under way at two-fifteen. "We're here today to see the bodily resurrection of Wesley Parker, one of Jesus Christ's own," Larry told the assembled mourners. "Just like Lazarus, he will rise."

Larry's voice squeaked at first. Then he composed himself and commanded: "Wesley, rise up in the name of Jesus."

There was no response.

Futile efforts by others to coax the little boy back to this life continued for a very long while. It was almost seven when the undertaker gently suggested it was time to give up and go home.

The next morning Wesley's body was buried without ceremony in Mountain View Cemetery.

Manslaughter Charges

Less than a week later, a police officer knocked at the door of the Parkers' home. "We've investigated your son's death and have come to place you and your wife under arrest," he said to Larry. The charge was manslaughter and child abuse. After a thirteen-week trial by jury the Parkers were found guilty on both counts. They were good parents—decent, compassionate, law-abiding people of genuine faith in Christ. But they lost the son they dearly loved because presumptuousness contaminated their faith, going beyond God's specific promises and leaving wisdom behind. The law looked upon them as felons, and the penalty for their crime could be as much as twenty-five years in prison.

Instead, the judge placed both of the parents on five years' probation and later reduced the charge to misdemeanor status and overturned the conviction. He felt no punishment by the court could equal the heartache the Parkers had inflicted on themselves.

Today, Larry and Lucky are free of the stigma of a felony conviction. They believe Wesley has forgiven them, and they are confident God has too. It may be a long time, however—and there is the lingering tragedy—before they are able to forgive themselves.

Misguided Theology

The Parkers' story sounds a sober warning against the earnest but misguided theology which regards as symbols of unbelief the use of medicines and other physical remedies to treat a variety of human frailties. A special vulnerability may lurk for Christians who move recklessly beyond the limits of God's written promises, intent upon securing for themselves a special power and a more comfortable life.

This book sounds the alarm for those convinced—however sincerely—that God must bless His people always with radiant health, success, and unfailing prosperity, provided only that we possess *enough faith* and make *positive confession.*

Stan Schmidt, a Jew, came to Christ after ten years as a diagnosed, lithium-regulated manic-depressive. During most of that decade, at least when he followed his medical regimen, he functioned normally and without episodes of depression. Then he experienced spiritual rebirth in response to the personal testimony, prayers, and concern of Christian friends. Some of these friends were firm in the notion that taking medicine or suffering a physical infirmity reflects sin, unbelief, or satanic interference.

Some of Stan's mentors were passionately convinced that Christ's gospel, for those who truly believe, includes the healing of all the body's ailments. "By His stripes," they reminded him from Isaiah 53, "we are *healed*, the *body* not just the soul." Basing their theology upon scriptural fragments, they insisted that believers must demonstrate their faith by claiming and receiving God's gift of deliverance. "If you *name* it," Stan's friends assured him, "then God says you have a right to *claim* it."

This mind-set assumes wealth, popularity, health, and emotional well-being are available to all who possess sufficient faith. Some teach these blessings can be claimed and experienced only by a superior category of Christians—the most likely candidates being those schooled under *their* prophetic ministry. They speak of a bold confidence in God that earns special influence. Others insist *all* believers are entitled to demand these blessings from a Father who longs to make His children prosper. It would be interesting to observe the reaction to that prosperity doctrine from a humble believer eking out a sparse living in a third-world country, thatched-roof village!

As several of his teachers told newly converted Stan Schmidt, the demons of his manic-depressive syndrome, controlled until that time by daily doses of lithium carbonate, are compelled to cringe before the demands of his newfound faith. "Medicine is of the devil," Schmidt heard again and again. "It is a crutch of unbelief," one of his teachers insisted. They explained how looking to medicine instead of relying upon the Lord Jesus to bring a long-term physical-chemical imbalance under control showed lack of faith and played into the devil's hands. Convinced that all believers can resolve their health difficulties by binding Satan or casting out demons, they consider recurring medical problems *prima facie* evidence of sin or unbelief.

This circular reasoning seems strangely reminiscent of the stand taken by Korean followers of a cult leader of the early sixties called Elder Kim. Declaring himself a prophet of God, the discredited Presbyterian elder established a Millennial City between Seoul and Inchon. A disenchanted follower told TEAM missionaries that all true believers who joined his flock were assured they would never die. Kim's followers considered themselves the only authentic Christians, other less enlightened churchmen being only pretenders to the faith. In return for receiving their hope of eternal life—a hope rooted mainly in Kim's own supposed prophetic influence with God—thousands deeded to this charismatic personality all their earthly possessions, moved into the Millennial City, and went to work in Kim's caramel and shirt factories confident of their indestructibility.

True believers, the self-styled prophet assured them, do not and cannot die. "Oh, now and then an *unbeliever* among us departs this life," his lieutenants acknowledged to TEAM missionaries when explaining the occasional shrouded body carted from the Millennial City. "But by this we know the dead one is not a true believer, for true believers never die." Circular reasoning is seldom the path to truth and reality. Later exposed, Kim ended up doing hard time in a Korean prison.

Depression: Number One Illness

The affliction which challenged Stan Schmidt's faith touches a broad spectrum in our nation's population. The precise reasons for the onset of this imbalance are obscure, but genetics are assumed to be an important factor. In many cases the symptoms of depression are easily recognizable.

People who suffer recurrent severe depression without corresponding highs are referred to medically as victims of a *unipolar* disorder. For them the mood swings go only downward. Feelings of defeat and despair become chronic. No amount of reasoning seems capable of penetrating this shell of imagined worthlessness and deeply rooted cynicism.

In contrast, *bipolars* (manic-depressives) veer from periods of elation, hyperactivity, and grandiose schemes on the up side to periods of guilt and sometimes suicidal despondency on the down side. In the depths of despair they find themselves unable to experience pleasure or to think rationally. When at their peaks, their behavior may be impulsive in the extreme. Operating irrationally under delusions of grandeur, many of them end up on the wrong side of the law, no longer able to distinguish clearly between wrong and right.

Even in Biblical Times

There is evidence this disorder is nothing new. Some theorize it was on record in the Old Testament nearly four thousand years ago. Even the rugged, tested, and proven deliverer, Moses, may have experienced mood swings which caused him at times to act out of character. We must not presume to look across the intervening millennia and pronouce him a manic-depressive, but Moses did destroy his status with the pharoahs by killing an Egyptian overseer he discovered bullying a Hebrew slave (see Exodus 2:12). Loyalty to his own kin and frustration with his adoptive royal family may have motivated that reckless act, but his impulsive action cost him dearly during the forty years which followed. With or without a physical hindrance, though, Moses, because he was indeed a man of faith, was always available to do what God commanded.

Moses' cry seems to reflect symptoms of depression, however: "I cannot carry all these people by myself; the burden is too heavy for me. If this is how you are going to treat me, put me to death right now—if I have found favor in your eyes—and do not let me face my own ruin" (Numbers 11:14–15). Similar death wishes are not unknown among frustrated people in our day and time.

Remember King Saul's murderous fits of anger? Plagued by "evil spirits from the Lord" (see 1 Samuel 16:14), he struck out not only against guileless David but also against Jonathan, his son. Saul's moods vascillated. One moment would find him arrogantly hostile toward people of proven loyalty, and the next would find him deep in a fit of depression, blaming himself and begging for forgiveness. Scripture also records the possibility of demonic influence in the king's fits of rage. In the end even David's harp, flute, and psalms could not soothe Saul's troubled spirit. The destructive Benjaminite is Biblical history's most clear-cut case of manic-depression. Still, he does not stand alone in the scriptural record. Jonah, Job, Elijah, and even the great King David are among Old Testament characters who cried for permission to die.

Down Through History

Across the centuries the symptoms of this affliction appear. Historians report that King George III suffered violent mood swings which today might be considered symptoms of bipolar depression. His blatantly faulty judgment while mishandling the American colonial crisis may have cost England its New World.

The life-style of Honoré de Balzac was typically manic, as were the style and the impulsiveness of his writings. He was characteristically *up*. If he suffered cycles of depression, they are not evident in his life or his work. He wrote *Cousin Bette* in an incredibly short six weeks. His orgies of work alternated with orgies of pleasure. He wrote ninety novels and stories in which some two thousand major characters appear. For two years before he died he shared with Mme. Evelina Hanska her estate in the Ukraine after pursuing her frantically from one end of Europe to the other. Finally he married the beauty and took her back to Paris. Three months later, at the age of fifty-one, de Balzac died in an apparent state of manic exhaustion.

Composer Robert Schumann produced music only during what are now recognized as his manic episodes. The years 1840 and 1849 were peaks of production for the German genius, and his contemporaries described him as "elated" during both of those cycles. When periods of deep depression engulfed him, he wrote nothing. In 1850 he was named music director for the town of Dusseldorf, but "mental illness" forced him to resign in 1854. That same year Schumann tried to drown himself in the Rhine but was foiled when a passer-by rescued him. He was then committed to an insane asylum near Bonn where he remained until his death two years later.

Mood swings plague creative people in a special way. Writers Virginia Wolf, Vachel Lindsay, and John Berryman all chose to escape their depression by committing suicide. Dylan Thomas, Thomas Wolfe, and F. Scott Fitzgerald probably did the same thing, only they used alcohol instead of pills or guns.

With a self-inflicted shotgun blast through his brain Ernest Hemingway revealed to the world the pathological gravity of the bipolar dysfunction which slowly consumed him in his later years. This accomplished and celebrated author had the literary world at his feet, but attacks of melancholia made his life increasingly intolerable. During his manic cycles he used his cranked-up energies to travel, write, hike, fish, and hunt. Yet in a violent fit of despondency when he was sixty-one years old and at the peak of his career, he chose to bring his life to a violent end.

Nothing more ominously defines the potentially tragic consequences of depression, America's number one illness.

Among Christians. But what of Christians through the years? Does their faith in Christ—the presence of the Holy Spirit in their hearts and minds—prevent them from falling victim to mood swings?

Apparently faith or lack of it makes little differ- ence. In fact, through the years some of Christendom's most energetic leaders have left be- hind evidence of emotional highs and lows. The re- former, Martin Luther, seemed to many of his era emotionally unstable, particularly in his cruel and unremitting attacks on Jews. England's prince of preachers, Charles Haddon Spurgeon, in his declin- ing years struggled through frequent bouts with de- pression. Even early in his ministry he described the "utter darkness of soul" which now and then settled upon him, leading him to doubt everything and even to fear he had "sunken into the abyss of unbelief." One of his early sermons includes this description of what could well be bipolar experiences:

> At certain periods, clouds and darkness cover the sun, and he beholds no clear shining of the day- light but walks in darkness. Now there are many who have basked in the sunshine of God for a sea- son . . . and suddenly—in a month or two—find that glorious sky is clouded. Instead of "green pas- tures" they have to tread the sandy desert; in place of "still waters" they find streams brackish to their taste and bitter to their spirit.

Spurgeon was called to the pulpit of London's new Park Street Chapel when he was barely twenty years old. Only eight years later, his congregation completed the huge Metropolitan Tabernacle to ac- commodate the crowds he attracted. But Spurgeon's biographers reveal the great preacher's dark secret: at times, particularly in the decade before he died, he found life scarcely worth the struggle.

By the winter of 1869 his health was failing. Smallpox, gout, and lung problems had taken their toll. His congregation allowed him the entire winter to recuperate in the warmer climate of Italy, but he was burdened by a deep concern for the ministry at the Tabernacle. His wife had become an invalid and a source of additional anxiety. He had been drawn into controversy by denouncing fellow Baptists' alleged departure from Biblical faith, and many friends, including clergymen trained in his Pastor's College, took sides against him. His was doubtless a reactive depression, but Spurgeon's firm Calvinistic faith did not exempt him from mood swings.

Spurgeon's favorite hymn—and one sung by a small group of worshipers the last time he taught in his living room—was "The Sands of Time are Sinking." Its last verse reads:

> I've wrestled on toward heaven
> 'Gainst storm and wind and tide.
> Now like a weary traveller
> That leaneth on his guide,
> Amid the shades of evening
> While sinks life's lingering sand
> I hail the glory dawning
> In Immanuel's land.

Among presidents. America's presidents also have suffered their share of mood swings. Abraham Lincoln's periods of depression are documented in his correspondence, in news stories from Civil War days, and in records left behind by those who knew him intimately. Historians are in accord that he was a melancholy man. His alternating periods of profound depression and aggressive achievement support the theory that he, too, may have suffered a chemical imbalance. Likely this resulted in manic-depressive symptoms which our revered sixteenth president managed not only to tolerate but also to incorporate as strengths.

When Lincoln was twenty-nine, the death of his first love, Ann Rutledge, plunged the young country lawyer into what appears to have been a period of deep depression. He was often seen wandering along the banks of the river near his home, seemingly filled with profound grief. Later in life, his personal physician, Dr. Anson Henry, noted and recorded his patient's occasional lack of energy, obsessive introversion, and indecisiveness. From law partner and biographer, William H. Herndon, we learn the bizarre details of Lincoln's early abortive attempt at marriage (*Life of Lincoln*, Quality Paperbacks, 1983). In 1841, on the day Lincoln and Mary Todd first planned to be united, the troubled groom failed to appear for the ceremony. His friends were shocked and embarrassed. Later, they found him walking alone, reportedly almost inconsolable in his depression. He simply hadn't the courage to go through with the wedding, though later he managed to endure it.

One collection of Lincoln's letters to friends includes this probably authentic though somber description of his mental outlook:

> I am now the most miserable man living. If what I feel were equally distributed to the whole human family, there would not be one cheerful face on earth. Whether I shall ever be better, I cannot tell; I awfully forebode I shall not. To remain as I am is impossible. I must die or be better, it appears to me.

Dr. Ronald R. Fieve, pioneer of lithium therapy in America and founder of the Foundation for Depression and Manic Depression, hypothesizes that Lincoln did indeed suffer a form of bipolar manic-depression. In spite of that apparent handicap, however, historians properly credit "Honest Abe" with saving our nation from the disaster of a permanent split.

Theodore Roosevelt's flamboyant personality was worlds apart from Lincoln's; he was anything but melancholy. The heights of Teddy's chronic elation are in stark contrast to the depths of Lincoln's depression. At times he was seen as a man possessed. Hyperactive and precocious as a child, he gained a reputation in college as an impulsive and obsessive monopolizer of every conversation. Later, his frenetic activities in the White House confounded staid Washingtonians. His inexhaustible energies frustrated those who attempted to work by his side. A visiting Briton described Roosevelt as "an interesting combination of St. Vitus and St. Paul." That, by the way, would constitute an acceptable lay definition for the cyclic phases of a bipolar personality.

Though Winston Churchill was known to be frenetic during much of his public life, it seems he also fought severe spells of melancholy. His biographer, Sir Charles Wilson, says that when depression struck the prime minister made little effort to hide it. Sarah Churchill writes that her father, "despite his eulogies, accolades and honors, still had a void in his heart . . . which no achievement or honor could completely fulfill." Armed solely with available biographical records, psychiatrists would likely consider Britain's wartime prime minister a classical, though unquestionably functional, case of manic-depression.

In 1972, the belated revelation of a history of depression and electroshock treatments drove Senator Thomas

Eagleton from the vice presidential spot on the Democrats' national slate. Presumably the revelation would have less effect today. Two decades ago, however, the stigma of mental illness was alive and toxic.

2

OUT OF THE PADDED CELL

When my mailbox at college coughed up the results of my first midterm exams in 1972, I sensed the party was just about over. There was nothing as high as a "D" to comfort Stan Schmidt, one of the most insecure freshmen on the university's roster.

My patient parents were in for yet another disappointment. I was failing every subject, which came as no surprise. At the ripe old age of eighteen I was making my first venture from the restrictions of a Jewish home and family. I had plunged wholeheartedly into my new freedom. Let the bookworms do the studying! Sure, my lack of motivation bothered me slightly on the rare occasions when my mind wandered to possible consequences. But readily available booze and party girls left little time for clear thinking. In addition, I had made an intriguing discovery called *pot*. Shutting myself in my dormitory room to light up a joint—easily accessible on most campuses—seemed considerably more exciting than quests for knowledge at the library. Marijuana became my faithful friend and promised relief for rapidly worsening bouts with alternating moods. *It might even help my grades,* I reasoned when doubts about the dope arose.

It was disturbing when the party ground to a halt, but it was crushing when the *nightmare* began. My feelings were soon swinging between euphoric grandeur on the "up" days and paranoid despondency on the "down." I did a lot of my brooding in secret, however, and seldom revealed my feelings to anyone else. Hallucinations haunted me even when there was no pot to smoke. I began to fear a secret enemy sought to kill me. Frequently I found myself imagining some compelling task must be done at once, yet frustrated because I couldn't manage to do it. I seemed incapable of establishing or achieving any goal that made sense. Increasingly I saw myself as a campus loner—a mystery man, rejected and sinking further each day into a darkening world of uncertainty, suspicion, fear, and failure.

When the inevitable happened and the dean's dismissal notice arrived, I blamed unseen conspirators for my academic failure. Sent packing by the college on a "medical discharge," I returned to Pittsburgh to pick up the pieces. My parents checked me into a hospital for tests—a psychiatric hospital. There I was diagnosed as paranoid and given a combination of tranquilizers and antidepressant medicines. I was also informed I wouldn't be allowed to leave the hospital until my parents decided I was ready to go. That incarceration lasted for just two weeks, however, because my parents finally relented and authorized my release, reclassified as an out-patient in psychotherapy. Two weeks after that, I decided I was as rational as the people who were treating me. Besides,

I was embarrassed by the *mental patient* tag. I canceled my sessions at the hospital and determined to restructure my life on my own terms.

For an unstabilized manic-depressive, however, that restructuring is seldom completed. For most, a life free from mood swings remains a phantom goal, tantalizing but always beyond reach. On one hand is a driving force which allows few silent or idle moments; on the other hand is the recurring doom and gloom of self-accusation, regret, and hopelessness. Unable to find a balance between the two, I swallowed my pride and sought help twice in other psychiatric hospitals. I dabbled again in antidepressants and tranquilizers, but my turmoil never left me. Unable to keep jobs and supported financially by my parents, I was making full speed ahead in the fast lane, increasingly infatuated with drugs and alcohol. Briefly in 1976 I moved to Florida with my family, but soon tired of what seemed a boring, sedentary life. I returned alone to Pittsburgh where the nightmare only worsened.

To this day I cannot explain it, but for unknown reasons I fantasized I had acquired two hundred thousand dollars from some mysterious source. Confident of my new wealth, I actually entered that amount in my checkbook and set out to live accordingly. Clothing stores, car rental agencies, expensive restaurants, and other businesses soon discovered I was fleecing them. Before prosecution could begin, though, a lady physician and friend of mine called my parents in Florida and informed them their son was sick. She saw my behavioral patterns growing increasingly irresponsible and bizarre. The dear woman made reservations for me and a friend on a southbound flight and suggested my parents take me directly to a psychiatric hospital when we arrived.

"Suppose he won't go?" my mother asked, remembering my fits of stubbornness.

"Then if I were you I'd have him arrested," the doctor said ominously. "If you don't, someone else probably will."

Though I am Jewish I had never given religion much thought. On the way to the airport, however, as my friend, Regis, drove me past St. Paul's cathedral, it occurred to me that God—if, indeed, there is such a being—might be willing to help me out of this snake pit. "Hold it right here for a minute, will you?" I asked impulsively. As the car ground to a halt I leaped out and dashed into the cathedral. With a sense of unreality I found myself in one of the pews, kneeling in prayer and crying out to God, whoever and wherever He was, to keep me from slipping further into this dark and forbidding vortex.

Suddenly I felt a touch upon my shoulder and heard a voice saying almost in a whisper, "Sir . . . er, young man, here's something for you. Just take this, okay . . . please?" When I turned, I was looking into the face of a littly old lady, a total stranger. She was offering words of consolation while extending a crucifix and a rosary from her open hand. "Take these, huh?" she repeated.

Hesitantly—and suspiciously—accepting the gift, I hung the crucifix around my neck, then looked up to thank the lady, but she was gone. For a long time after that I wore the crucifix, more as a fetish than anything else. I preferred that people think of me as anything but religious.

Barely making the flight before the gate closed, Regis and I found our seats on the jet and buckled our seatbelts. Even before we reached cruising altitude I showed him my checkbook with the two hundred thousand dollar deposit, but my question betrayed my insecurity. "Do you think I'm sick?" I asked.

"Yeah, I think you probably are, Stan," was his honest reply. "But don't worry, I'm praying for you. The Lord is going to work all this out, so just sit back and relax." I wasn't real sure how the Lord was going to fit into this puzzle, but the words made me feel better. I relaxed so well that I slept the rest of the way to Miami.

When Regis and I arrived in Florida, hospital wasn't what I had in mind. Even though my parents wanted to enroll me in a therapeutic program immediately, I was convinced that wasn't necessary. After all, I had work to do; I had to distribute the better part of my two hundred thousand dollars where it would do the most good. My policy was simple: if people seemed to need help, then part of my bonanza was theirs. The truth is, I also liked to spread my charity now and then to people who *didn't* need help, just so they'd know a real philanthropist when they saw one.

My brother, John, was cagey. He didn't believe my story of instant wealth. My cousin, Bruce, also had doubts, especially when I wrote a worthless twenty-five thousand dollar check to help him with a business venture. Finally, on the day after Christmas I was hauled, protesting, to a psychiatric hospital—a move encouraged, no doubt, by my announcement that I was thinking about converting to Christianity. Not that I understood what Christianity was all about, but I couldn't get the little old lady off my

mind, and the crucifix and rosary seemed appropriate tools for changing religions.

So I was off to the hospital. Before agreeing to
admit me, though, a staff physician placed me in an
isolation room with my mother and monitored our
conversation through a one-way mirror and hidden
microphone.

"Mom, I think I'll buy new cars for those two
nurses who checked me in," I told her, not knowing
that the doctor watched and listened. To me, buying
the cars seemed a stroke of genius. "Don't you think
the girls are nice?"

"Yes, son, they're nice, but they don't need new
cars, so keep your money," she dismissed the idea.

"It's *my* money," I remember saying stubbornly.
"I've got a hundred and fifty thousand left, and I'll
spend it any way I want." Then, half to Mom and
half to myself, "I'll bet they'd appreciate new cars."

"Sure, son," was all my mother could think of saying. She shook her head sadly. "Sure," she said again.

After that exchange it didn't take much monitor-
ing to convince the psychiatrist I needed help.

"What's the idea of the bracelet?" I said when one
of those two nice nurses slipped a plastic name-band
around my wrist.

"Oh, I'll bet you'd like to stay with us for a
while," she said airily, as if she were talking to a
five-year-old.

"I'll be okay," I objected, pulling my arm away.
What gave these people the right to treat me like a
child? "I don't need a bracelet, thank you."

"I know," she replied, slipping the name-band in
place in spite of my protests. "You'll be just fine. All

right? But now we'll just say 'bye-bye' to Mother for a little while and I'll take you to your room. Okay?"

"Don't worry, son," my mom said as she patted me on the head. "It's just for a couple of days, probably. So go with the nice nurse."

"Sure, Mom," I tossed over my shoulder as the young lady wheeled my chair down the long hall. The pressure was on, but I figured I could use a little rest. I called as the distance between us lengthened, "Don't worry, Mom. The doctors will see there's nothing wrong with me, and you can come get me tomorrow."

Only a moment later, I noticed the *Closed Unit* sign as the nurse wheeled me into an admittance room and secured the heavy door behind us. Inside, another attendant asked me routine questions about razor blades, pocket knives, nail files, and belts, then reached for the crucifix around my neck.

"Are you afraid I'll kill myself?" I asked her, lifting my hands to protect that valuable religious fetish.

"It's my job," the attendant answered, trying again.

"Take the g-d thing off his miserable neck," barked a big, rough-looking guy seated in one of the straight-back wooden chairs. Until that moment he had been just another patient, watching in silence.

"Yeah?" I bristled. "You want to try?" People don't make comments like that around Stanley Schmidt and get away with it.

"You wanna stop me?" the big guy retorted, leaping to his feet and lunging at me and my crucifix.

Angrily, I rose to the defense of my treasure and a battle royal began. Unable to separate us, the nurses flashed the hospital's *rainbow* code, warning of an emergency and summoning security. Soon several muscular psychiatric aides and security guards burst into the unit. In a matter of seconds my attacker and I found ourselves in restraints. The rough-looking guy was hustled in one direction, and I in my wheelchair was rolled away in another. Within moments I was wheeled into a room lined with rubber padding. There they placed me none too gently upon a narrow bed, strapped me in a prone position and heavily sedated me.

Groggy as I was, it began to dawn upon me that either the world was a tragically cruel and unjust place or I must be a very sick man. After thinking it over for a while I decided both were probably true!

Unable to move, all I could do was cry out in protest. Since no one responded, I decided to cry out to God, whoever and wherever He was. The words came in a croaking voice only God could understand. Suddenly, though, I felt like someone or something had entered the room. Whether fantasy—a mere slice of my hallucinations—or something supernatural, the reader will have to determine for himself. I saw two arms and hands partly covered by a draping white robe above the foot of my bed. In the hands I saw a huge cross, but I was looking at it through a mist. What I saw was surreal, beautiful, and powerful. Then a sense of peace and assurance came over me, and in spite of those restraints I fell asleep.

The next morning I was released from the padded cell. "I'd like to have a Bible, please," I said to the nurse who pushed me down the hall to my new quarters. I had decided to spend my hospital stay exploring the book so many people feel is actually the Word of God.

"Now, Stan," she purred, "the doctor says you shouldn't be so preoccupied with religion. We'll just get you something else to read, okay?" Her report on my condition that day reads:

> Patient continues grandiose and religiously preoccupied. Attitude calmer today. Patient states he had a vision which he interpreted to be Christ telling him not to take his medicine. Encouraged him to take medicine as ordered by physician. Wants to read Bible, but encouraged him not to do so at present. Manipulative.

* Manipulative or not, what I remember most clearly is that I kept insisting until I got my Bible!

ﳂ   ﳂ   ﳂ

Melancholia: Friend or Foe?

Robert Burton, English churchman and scholar nearly four centuries ago, was plagued by mood swings. He was vicar of St. Thomas Church at Oxford in the early seventeenth century and keeper of the college library. An intense man, Burton possessed a consuming interest in medicine, literature, history, theology, and science. Not unlike others classified, though perhaps arbitrarily, as "unconventional," Burton was a man of unusual gifts, not the least of which was an extraordinary memory. He was known for his great skill at systematizing facts and keeping detailed research records. In addition, his associates at Oxford regarded him as an eloquent and witty man, though something of a recluse. In forty-five years as vicar and librarian Burton reportedly never ventured beyond the borders of the college town. He was too busy pursuing with passionate curiosity the various aspects of knowledge accessible in his library!

But another and more somber reason for his nonconformity emerges from his writings. Burton left only one publication of note, printed when he was forty-four, and though he poured into it a rich mixture of classical and curious learning, he chose to title his book of poems *The Anatomy of Melancholy*, (3 vols. A. R. Shilleto, ed., New York: AMS Printing, Inc., 1621). In it he makes this revealing observation:

> If there is a hell on earth, it is to be found
> in a melancholy man's heart.

Then, shifting into poetic gear, he writes:

> I'll change my state with any wretch
> Thou canst from good or dungeon fetch.
> My pain's past cure, another Hell,
> I may not in this torment dwell,
> Now desperate I hate my life,
> Lend me a halter or a knife.
> All my griefs to this are jolly
> Naught so damned as melancholy.

Burton apparently was no stranger to bipolar mood swings, though scientific identification of manic-depressive symptoms would not come for centuries. He wrote not only of the darkness of his bouts with depression but also, in dramatic contrast, of the almost pathological excitement he experienced when stimulated by his manic moods:

I'll not change life with any king.
I ravished am: can the world bring
More joy than still to laugh and smile
In pleasant toys time to beguile?
Do not, O do not trouble me,
So sweet content I feel and see
All my joys to this are folly.
None so divine as melancholy. . . .
None so sweet as melancholy.

"None so damned" in one verse; "none so divine" and "none so sweet" in the next! Perhaps the poet, Milton, meant something similar when, during the same century, he wrote in his *Il Penseroso* the seemingly contradictory salute, "Hail divinest Melancholy."

If that seems surprisingly insightful for the seventeenth century, consider the words of Roman philosopher Caelius Aurelianus who informed us a full twelve centuries before that:

The signs of approaching melancholy are . . . anguish and distress, dejections, silence, animosity . . . sometimes a desire to live, and at other times a longing for death.

Melancholia has many forms—or, as psychiatrist John White puts it in his book titled *Masks of Melancholy* (Downer's Grove: InterVarsity Press, 1982), it "wears many masks." Each form likely has been given a medical name, but learning to recite depression's names or identify its masks seems an inappropriate challenge for melancholia's victims. It is enough to know that no one is likely to experience precisely the same symptoms other victims report. The important thing to remember is the possibility that even in the worst cases of depression the problem may be a chemical imbalance and a physical dysfunction rather than a mental illness.

Diagnosis of Depression

The bad news is that depression is the most common of all mental problems; the good news is that it is considered the most treatable. For reasons unknown, depression affects women two-and-a-half times more often than men. One woman in four can expect to develop a form of depression during her lifetime, while only one man in ten will be affected. On the brighter side, nearly 90 percent of those who suffer from depression can be effectively treated.

The proper verb form here is *can* be. Lamentably, nearly 80 percent of depression's victims fail to recognize their affliction and seek the treatment which could alleviate their suffering. Out of ignorance, some fail to link their episodes and detect the pattern into which they have fallen. For others, the reason may be reluctance to face reality. Instead, they describe their physical symptoms as being "not quite with it today" or "a little bit out of sorts." They may attribute their mood swing to "a bug of some kind," to lack of sleep, to stress on the job, or perhaps to changed eating habits. Some are genuinely concerned about their emotional stability but are unwilling to seek help for fear of the stigma of consulting a "shrink."

The fact that depression's symptoms are so handily, and often mistakenly, attributed to other causes contributes to the difficulty in diagnosing and treating the dysfunction. People tend to deny the existence of depression by insisting, "After what I've gone through I've got a right to act this way," or "You'd be dragging the ground too if you had to work with the turkeys I work with." Actually, there can be legitimate environmental, circumstantial, and reactive reasons for feelings of depression, and when we encounter such causes it should surprise no one that melancholia strikes. But persistent depression may constitute a good reason for talking it over with someone qualifed to provide reliable answers.

What Are the Symptoms?

Depression is usually characterized by pervasive feelings of sadness, a deep-down helplessness and hopelessness, and a noticeably worsening irritability. The National Depressive and Manic-Depressive Association (NDMDA) suggests seeking professional help whenever a person experiences four or more of the following symptoms continually for more than two weeks:

- Noticeable change of appetite, with either significant weight loss or weight gain, even though not dieting.

- Noticeable change in sleeping patterns, such as fitful sleep, inability to sleep, or sleeping too much.

- Loss of interest, lack of pleasure in activities formerly enjoyed.

- Loss of energy and notable fatigue.

- Feelings of worthlessness.

- Persistent feelings of hopelessness.

- Feelings of inappropriate guilt.

- Inability to concentrate or think; indecisiveness.

- Recurring thoughts of death or suicide, wishing to die, or suicide attempts.

- Overwhelming feelings of sadness and grief, accompanied by waking at least two hours earlier than normal in the morning, feeling depressed, and moving significantly slower.

- Disturbed thinking, a severe symptom developed by depressed persons.

Many victims of depression—perhaps some reading these words—feel mental and physical symptoms like these follow them day and night. For them, good news or enjoyable events cannot reduce the level of personal anxiety and despair. No end seems in sight. Many victims are so fettered and disabled by their feelings that they cannot summon either the courage or the energy to make an appointment with a professional who might help them. Even if a friend or loved one makes the appointment for them, they may refuse to keep it, pleading that their case is so hopeless there seems no point in wasting the time or the money. If a pill were offered, guaranteed to relieve their symptoms, some might be so deeply entrenched in their misery, it wouldn't seem worth the effort to swallow the medicine.

Those concerned for such victims may willingly offer advice, encouragement, and support at first, but sooner or later they are bogged down by discouragement. Many quietly withdraw, and when they do, the depressed person is more alone than ever. Nevertheless, he or she isn't buying the advice anyway, doesn't appreciate the help offered, and turns a deaf ear to any effort to provide comfort. Therapists who work with the NDMDA urge persistence, however, on the part of those inclined to help. If their helpers don't give up, most victims sooner or later will take steps to deal with their problem.

Who Is Afflicted?

England's redoubtable Samuel Johnson wrote candidly of his problems with depression. He informed readers in the late eighteenth century, "I inherited a vile melancholy from my father, which has made me mad all my life, at least not sober." That "vile melancholy" need not prove, however, that Johnson was sick or suffered a chemical imbalance. The melancholy could have been an understandable reaction to his personal circumstances. He may have felt himself entitled to a sour disposition because of his reported mottled complexion, myopia, and awkward movements. The ungainly appearance and eccentric behavior described by his biographers probably made Samuel Johnson the target of cruel jokes during his youth. Historians picture him as a hypochondriac with a morbid fear of death. He suffered from prolonged fits of absentmindedness and was slovenly in his habits as well as in his appearance. Perhaps he had a right to claim moments of melancholy.

Isn't it true that the most winsome among us feel "blue" or "down in the dumps" at times, often with anxiety that boasts no name? Transitory feelings of discouragement or sadness are considered quite normal, especially the period termed *reactive depression* during or immediately following disappointment or tense and trying circumstances. Our Bibles teach us we are flawed products of a fallen universe. As long as we remain human we will be forced to acknowl-

edge not only our imperfections but also the imperfections of others, including other Christians. Things
don't always go the way we had hoped or expected or
even prayed. So all of us have our ups and downs and
indulge in commiserating with ourselves. More serious
problems surface only when we fail to recover from
those feelings in a reasonable length of time. If we still
exhibit symptoms of melancholy two or three weeks
after adverse circumstances, we should suspect we are
suffering from some version of the dysfunction known
as depression.

Be aware that depression is not the peculiar curse
of the adult. It can appear at any age, even in infants.
Single, brief, and isolated episodes of severe depression may occur at any stage of life. If they have occurred once, they may occur again. Available research
data suggests that approximately half the people who
suffer a single episode are fated to have others. Some
victims have episodes that are separated by several
years, while others experience clusters of the attacks
over relatively brief periods. Between crippling episodes of depression or manic-depression, many victims manage to function normally. For a fortunate few
the affliction may disappear as unceremoniously as it
appeared. Occasionally a spontaneous and permanent
remission occurs for no clear reason; the cloud just
lifts to descend no more.

Whatever the symptoms, however, it is crucially
important that the victim seek professional help.
Roughly 25 percent of those who suffer chronic depression remain untreated by a qualified medical
doctor and find themselves unable to maintain normal routines. Job, marriage, and other relationships

are often jeopardized if treatment is not sought. The word of wisdom, then, is "get help."

The Faith-Healing Question

When confronted by threats to health or well-being, the thoughts of many Christians turn naturally to faith healing. God certainly knows our aversion to suffering, and doesn't He love us? We are confident He has the power and authority to heal. Isn't He omnipotent? He can perform any miracle that pleases Him. Can it be the will of a loving and powerful heavenly Father for people He calls His own to be handicapped by physical misfortune or hindered by adverse circumstances? Some believers find it difficult to accept negative answers to questions that arise so naturally in every mind. We must remind ourselves of the folly of answering those questions with human reasoning rather than from the revealed wisdom of the Word of God.

Gary and Margaret Hall made that mistake. Their twenty-six-day-old son died in 1984 after they followed the reasonings of their Indiana pastor, Hobart Freeman. They refused to take the sick baby to a doctor.

Under Indiana law, refusing medical care to a child is criminal. The state statute concedes "It is a defense that the accused person in the legitimate practice of his religious belief provided treatment through spiritual means through prayer in lieu of medical care to his dependents," but the clause didn't help the Halls. Two months after their indictment, an Indiana jury found them guilty of a felony.

Ditto David and Kathleen Bergmann. Their nine-month-old Allyson died of an untreated brain infection. "I didn't kill my daughter," Kathleen testified during her trial. "I gave her to the Lord." Their withholding of medical care was in obedience to Hobart Freeman and his Faith Assembly's stern prohibition against "satanically inspired" medical care. "When my daughter was going through the fever, I rebuked it," Kathleen testified. "I sat up all night long, and I quoted Scripture." The vigil didn't work. The next day the child died.

Fifteen-year-old Faith Assembly adherent Pamela Menne, refusing a dialysis regimen, died of kidney failure in her home. David and Nigal Oleson filed a multimillion dollar lawsuit against Faith Assembly, claiming Freeman and his associates brainwashed them. Then, as if in ironic benediction, Freeman himself died that year in his Shoe Lake home, despite his public claims that his purified faith exempted him from dying. The cult leader expired due to complications from untreated diabetes. Practicing to the end what he preached about the power of genuine faith, the self-styled prophet refused to seek medical help. The Old Testament has a relevant warning: "Do not listen to what the prophets are prophesying to you; they fill you with false hopes. They speak visions from their own minds, not from the mouth of the LORD" (Jeremiah 23:16).

Devilish Delusions

Freeman taught his followers that if their faith were strong and pure enough they would experience neither sickness nor death. His reasoning followed a curious line of presumption. Since salvation is only by faith in God, people exercising such faith need not get sick and thus must not trust in doctors and medicine. In Freeman's theological system illness, doctors, and medicines are devilish delusions to be denied and avoided.

Several deaths among families of the Indiana cult had warranted police investigation, beginning in 1980. Natail Joy Mudd and Bonnie Joe Vargo, both four years old, expired even though their parents exercised their faith by commanding Jesus to heal them. Freeman's own grandson, Brent Kinsey, died of respiratory complications shortly after his birth at home with no professional practitioner in attendance. In 1981 Betty Nel, the fifty-six-year-old follower of Freeman who donated the land for the church, came down with pneumonia and refused treatment. She succumbed when both lungs ceased functioning. To the end she held steadfastly to the church doctrine condemning doctors and medicine. Two years later, her husband's second wife died of breast cancer, untreated because of loyalty to Freeman's teaching.

In 1982, another Mudd child had a basketball-size tumor removed from her abdomen and later died. Between 1983 and 1986, the *Fort Wayne News-Sentinel* published a series of articles detailing the untimely deaths of *no less than fifty-two* of Freeman's followers in six states. These victims, or their parents acting for them, had shunned doctors and medicine in obedience to Faith Assembly's strict and highly presumptuous doctrines.

Hobart Freeman

Who, then, was this strange "prophet," teaching such presumptuous faith while exercising life-or-death control over his followers? "A religious monk with incredible power," one elderly member of his congregation described Hobart Freeman.

In 1942, he got a diploma from Bryant and Stratton Business College in Louisville, then moved to Florida to open a successful photography business and a profitable grocery store. "Everything I touched turned to money," he claimed in his recorded testimony. In 1950, however, his business ventures soured. After two years of frustration he was converted to Christ and felt called to the ministry of the gospel. In just three years he completed a four-year degree in Bible and history with an "A" average. From there he returned to Louisville and earned a Master of Theology degree at Southen Baptist Theological Seminary in 1956.

By this time, however, Freeman was becoming disenchanted with the Baptist denomination. With special vehemency he rejected Christianity's celebration of Christmas and Easter as being of pagan origin. "The life of faith" and "positive confession" became his obsessions. "I didn't work five minutes all the way through college or seminary," Freeman has testified. "We claimed everything by faith." That philosophy seems strangely in confict with the Apostle Paul's, expressed in 2 Thessalonians 3:6–10:

> In the name of the Lord Jesus Christ, we command you, brothers, to keep away from every brother who is idle and does not live according to the teaching you received from us. For you yourselves know how you ought to follow our example. We were not idle when we were with you, nor did we eat anyone's food without paying for it. On the contrary, we worked night and day, laboring and

toiling so that we would not be a burden to any of you. We did this, not because we do not have the right to such help, but in order to make ourselves a model for you to follow. For even when we were with you, we gave you this rule: "If a man will not work, he shall not eat."

After Freeman completed a Ph.D. degree in Old Testament and Hebrew at Grace Theological Seminary in Winona Lake, Indiana, the seminary hired him to teach in its Old Testament department.

His relationship with Grace Seminary soon deteriorated, however. Freeman's theology became more and more separatist, though at that point he was not yet teaching divine healing. He and his wife, Ruth, were soon neglecting their attendance at church services, preferring to provide for seminary students competing worship and teaching services in their home. More and more doctrinal differences surfaced which alienated him from other faculty members. In January 1962 the seminary bought up his contract and let him go.

By this time, however, the informal gathering in the Freeman home had taken the form of an organized church with its own doctrinal statement.

In 1966, Freeman attended McCormick Seminary in Illinois. There, Freeman was introduced to "the baptism of the Holy Spirit," an experience that revolutionized his approach to Scripture. For the first time, speaking in tongues, special revelations, supernatural visions, and divine healing became obsessions. The emphasis of Freeman's ministry shifted sharply under the influence of healing evangelists.

In 1978, Freeman erected a tent for his ministry on the plot of land near Goshen, Indiana, donated by one of his admirers. His popularity and influence grew so rapidly that by the end of that year his congregation constructed a brown metal structure to house Faith Assembly activities. The church purposed to "do it right" and not make the blatant mistakes institutionalized Christianity was making. Isolation intensified. Guards with walkie-talkies patrolled the Faith Assembly parking lot as protection against theft and vandalism. They also turned away nonmembers.

Freeman became a recognized authority on charismatic theology, and his writings and tapes were distributed across the nation. He published ten books, including a major volume on the Old Testament prophets published by the conservative and anything but charismatic Moody Press in Chicago.

"I have not spent a dime on medicine or medical care since the baptism of the Holy Spirit and receiving new insights into God's promise of healing," he once claimed. Still, Freeman had his share of health problems. As a child he contracted polio, which left him with a withered lower right leg. Prior to the baptism of the Holy Spirit, he had kidney surgery. He also suffered several heart attacks. But while his body was weak, he was blessed with what even his severest critics agree was a brilliant mind.

Powerful influence. Writing for the *Warsaw Times-Union*, John Davis, a former student of Freeman's at Grace Seminary, in a four-part series of articles on his former mentor printed September 27–30, 1983, suggested four reasons for the influence the strange man exerted over the trusting people of his flock:

1. His mastery of the Scriptures, which included knowledge of both Hebrew and Greek. His preaching was characterized by careful organization of material and frequent quotation of supporting Scripture. His people say they found his messages intriguing, exciting, and challenging.

2. His claim to supernatural visions and special revelations. He frequently provided for Faith Assembly members what he alleged to be direct, personal statements from God to support his theological views. No one in his congregation dared challenge him. To do so would be questioning God Himself.

3. Intimidation of his followers. Freeman often reminded his flock of divine curses and punishment reserved for those who dare fall away from the faith as taught at his assembly. When journalist Davis interviewed him, Freeman spoke pointedly of the way all reporters who criticized his ministry had eventually suffered illness, injury, or death—a friendly gesture to ensure his articles would be favorable to Freeman. They were not, but they were fair.

4. The isolation and discipline of Faith Assembly which forbids reading newspapers, watching television, and fellowshipping with members of other churches. That extreme separatist and obscurantist policy tends to discourage independent thought and guarantee uncritical commitment by Freeman's followers.

Positive confession creates reality. The heart of Faith Assembly's theological system is its "faith formula" assertion that when genuine faith is exercised by the believer and accompanied by a "positive confession," anything the believer sets out to accomplish can be achieved. God is obligated to heal *every* sickness in *every* circumstance when such faith is displayed. "When genuine faith is present," Freeman frequently reaffirmed, "it alone will be sufficient, for it will take the place of medicines and other aids." Confronted by instances in which followers of his teachings had not been healed or had even died, Freeman rationalized, "These results can be considered in some cases to be discipline or judgment on God's part. In other cases there has been a complete lack of faith."

Concerning the riddle of his own withered leg, Freeman offered a simple solution and a lesson in his concept of reality: "It has been healed," the *Times-Union* writer quotes him as insisting, "but God hasn't chosen to manifest it yet." A detached observer might inquire whether Freeman's delayed healing was discipline, judgment, or lack of faith. The prophet chose not to address the question. Associates called his delayed healing a "Job's trial" designed to enrich Freeman's ministry.

For people who reason in that way, a total distortion of reality is not surprising. Psychologists say such whimsical thinking is characteristic of blind followers of radical and unfounded doctrines. Whether the distortion is the cause or the effect, who can tell?

Freeman taught that reality is best identified in terms of faith, not vice versa. When healing isn't manifested, the believer may really be healed, but doubts and fears may for a short time make it seem he's still sick. The reality is that he is healed. "If you say 'I don't see any better,'" *Times-Union* writer John Davis says he told his trusting flock concerning problems with failing eyesight, "then it means you haven't come often enough to learn all the conditions. Don't take your glasses off until you're willing to break them, crush them, walk all over them." When believers can trample them underfoot and *then* confirm they've been healed, they are practicing Freeman's "positive confession." Visitors to Faith Assembly testify to seeing the faithful upon arrival carefully take off their eyeglasses and even remove their hearing aids before getting out of their cars, in order not to risk discipline at the hands of church leaders.

Concerning the reality of healing, Freeman argues in *Faith for Healing,* (Warsaw, IN: Faith Publications, 1974), "Sometimes it is a moment after; at other times it is a week, month, or longer, before the answer is seen in the visible realm. But true faith continues to confess that God has heard and granted our request and that we shall have it. We must always receive it in the faith realm before we shall ever see it in the natural or visible realm." He did not offer Biblical support for that somewhat fanciful doctrine.

In his book titled *Positive Thinking and Confession,* (Warsaw, IN: Faith Publications, 1974), Freeman provided this candid description of the way his "positive confession" doctrine works:

> I designate this process of the cultivation of the mind "spiritual brainwashing." Satan seems to have most Christians' minds filled with thoughts of doubt, fear, inability, insecurity, worry and defeat; therefore this negativism must be flushed out and the mind saturated with the positive Word of

the Lord before the Enemy can be forced to release
his hold on the mind and thoughts.

"We must practice thought control," he added with
considerable candor. "We must deliberately empty
our minds of everything negative concerning the person, problem or situation confronting us."

Safeguards

Still, in spite of inconsistencies, there seems no scar-
city of trusting people eager to follow charismatic
leaders who offer them absolutes, even absolutes that
have no basis in reality. Are there no safeguards to
prevent the falling of ordinary believers under the
spell of similarly fallacious reasoning? What can keep
us from the personal, spiritual devastation of presumptuous faith?

The sobering story of Hobart Freeman and his
Faith Assembly—not different, qualitatively, from
that of Jim Jones and his People's Temple—suggests
to us these practical guidelines:

1. We must guard against sifting through our Bibles searching for something that will confirm
what we've already decided or what we *want*
to be true.

2. We dare not forget that in His activity among
men God seeks *His* glory, not ours. Christ's
teaching aims at getting *us* to do what *God*
wants, not vice versa. His purpose for us
moves us toward spiritual prosperity and our
eternal destiny, not toward temporal benefits
like wealth, wellness, and carefree existence.

3. We must keep in mind the sobering fact that not all supernatural activity is of God. Physical healing and other miracles can take place through Satan's power as a means of distracting, misleading, entrapping, or destroying us. The Holy Spirit is not the only spirit at work in our world today.

4. We must discipline ourselves to be wary of doctrines or practices based upon fragments of Scripture. The mature believer should carefully explore the whole counsel of God in every matter, comparing Scripture with Scripture. We must establish what we believe only after it is confirmed in the Word of God. That God-breathed Word is the source of our doctrines, our reproof, our corrections, and our instruction in the lessons of life (see 2 Timothy 3:16).

5. We must practice a healthy skepticism toward claims of supernatural experiences. As in scientific research, the only reliable confirmation lies in observability and repeatability, and those are seldom possible. Even though the one who relates the experience is sincere, not all the healings and other miracles we hear described really happened. Human imagination and enthusiasm have few boundaries. "Sanctify them by the truth; your *Word* is truth" (John 17:17, emphasis added).

6. We must be leery of claims of special revelations, visions, voices, and other messages from God. He can work sovereignly in any way He pleases, but most claims of personal prophetic anointing prove presumptuous, self-serving,

and consequently dangerous. "Faith comes from hearing the message, and the message is heard through the Word of Christ" (Romans 10:17).

7. We need to understand the full scope of John the Baptist's "He must become greater; I must become less" (John 3:30). Religious people who appropriate glory, advantages, or benefits to themselves are not reliable guides to the mind and purposes of God.

8. We must be alert to the danger posed by manipulative or authoritative leaders. In God's kingdom His appointed leaders rule wisely and selflessly by serving. They do not "lord it over" (1 Peter 5:3) those entrusted to them; they seek nothing for themselves.

9. If we do not know or cannot find for ourselves the Scripture that supports a doctrine, we must be bold to ask. We need the courage to demand, "Where in the Bible is the basis for that?" Then we must read and decide for ourselves, armed with a reliable basis for determining the validity of the doctrine.

10. We must not forget that the faith we exercise is the gift of God (see Ephesians 2:9). It reflects no favoritism or superiority in God's sight. Beware of those preoccupied with the quality or quantity of their own faith.

3

A DISINTEGRATING WORLD

S tan, all of the tests point in the same direction, and we've . . . ah, agreed on a diagnosis," the psychiatrist explained as he leaned back in his chair across the desk from me and lowered the paper he'd been studying. He had my attention. "We're ready to say now you are suffering from a type of mental disorder." Then he added quickly, "One we consider treatable, I should say. We call it *manic-depressive psychosis*. Does that mean anything to you?" He seemed to be searching for words and phrases a nonmedical person might understand.

"You mean . . . I'm some kind of *lunatic?*" I asked.

"No, I'm saying you have a chemical imbalance—a defect in the way your body functions, like . . . well, like diabetes or arthritis, only . . ."

"Yeah, but you *are* saying I have a . . . a *mental* problem, right?" I interrupted, getting to my feet. "I'm sick, huh?" After the tricks my emotions were playing on me, I suspected as much, but I wasn't anxious to have those suspicions confirmed.

"No, I can't let you call it *sick*," the doctor insisted, waving me back into my chair. "It's biological,

Stan, and, yes, it does affect the brain's processes. If our chemistry gets fouled up, our body parts can't work right, okay? A part of you that's affected by this imbalance happens to be your brain. Your *brain*, right?—not your mind or your mentality. Do you see the difference?"

"Yeah? You tell me the difference." I was feeling a bit hostile by that time.

"The difference is that your mind isn't sick and you're not crazy," he countered. "Your mind is perfectly capable of functioning properly once we get the chemistry back in balance and keep it that way."

"And how do we do that?" I pressed.

"With medicine," the psychiatrist said matter-of-factly. "We've got a new drug to work with—one that's proved quite successful—and your symptoms seem made to order for it. But let me tell you that we're not going to abandon psychotherapy. That has a place in your healing too, but we're going to back it up with physiotherapy, which means in layman's language we'll also give you medicine."

"So what's the medicine?"

"Lithium carbonate," my doctor replied.

I'd heard of it, and had some ideas of my own. "That's still experimental, isn't it?" I asked. I had dug up information on it just in case. Lithium, the lightest of all metals, is found in combination with certain rock formations. Mental patients in this country had been taking the medicine since the early 1970s, and the results were considered encouraging, but I wasn't ready to be one of the psychiatric ward's guinea pigs.

"Research never stops, but lithium definitely has proven itself," the doctor explained. "There's plenty of data available to make it your best shot right now—maybe your *only* shot."

"Sorry, but I don't like the idea," I grunted. Now he had a stubborn and rebellious patient on his hands—stiffened back, jutted jaw, folded arms, and all.

"You don't get a choice," the doctor said bluntly, leaning forward on his desk. "You're in serious trouble, Stan," he added grimly, "and if we don't do something about it right away you're going to be in worse trouble still. Do you understand that? We want to get you well and out of here. So that's why you're starting on a lithium regimen today." He told me to go to the nurses' station and start my first dosage.

So, starting on lithium carbonate is precisely what I did, like it or not. As it happened, the improvement was prompt and dramatic. In fact, two weeks later the psychiatrist judged me stabilized sufficiently to release me from the hospital.

"When can I quit taking these pills?" I wanted to know.

"Maybe later, maybe never," my doctor responded cagily but candidly, then handed me a prescription. "We'll do a blood test several times a year and see how your lithium level reads. Probably your dosage will need adjusting now and then. But whether or not you're on lithium or any other medicine isn't the important thing—it's being stabilized and living a normal life. What's important is getting well, right?"

"If you say so," I replied glumly, and soon I was on my way home. In spite of my skepticism, for almost a decade after that I enjoyed a life increasingly normal in the areas that seemed to me most important—mentally, physically, and socially. Spiritually?

Well, that's a department I wasn't concerned about—
not then, at least. But apparently God *was* concerned.
Before long I was getting glimpses of His hand at
work in developing my spiritual consciousness as
well, though it wasn't in the way I would have
planned it.

A sudden downturn in my fortunes began in a
convenience store where someone had cut open a
case of merchandise and left the plastic bands in the
aisle. I stumbled clumsily over those bands and
wrenched my way to the concrete floor, injuring several lumbar and cervical vertebrae as I went down.
Unpleasant little adventures like that probably would
upset the balance of anyone's life, but it proved particularly traumatic for me. By that time I had opened
my own sporting goods store and married the girl I
had dated for five years. I considered myself an all-
around athlete, increasingly pleased with my ability
at softball, tennis, and anything else offering oppor-
tunities to compete. Business at my store was good.
In the social whirl, I saw myself as the life of the
party, particularly on the crest of a few drinks and a
joint or two of pot.

After my back injury, though, things started
downhill. Pain killers and sleeping pills took the
edge off my constant misery, but they didn't mix
well with the booze, the marijuana, and the lithium.
None of those things helped my marriage. My wife's
nursing career took more and more of her time, and I
wasn't exactly giving top priority to enhancing our
relationship. Every day seemed to bring new con-
flicts. I began to feel like a boxer in the ring suddenly
realizing he was hopelessly mismatched. The bell
rang to start round one each morning at my store,

where business was deteriorating, and round two began in the evening when I came home to a wife increasingly dissatisfied with her choice of a husband. This is not the environment in which bipolars thrive. Besides all that, I was getting careless about my daily doses, and that made me a sitting duck for a new episode of manic-depression.

Finally the first recurrence of my mood swings came, turning my entire world toward the "loss" column. I should have returned to my lithium regimen at the first sign of trouble, but I didn't. My business went into a tailspin, and it wasn't long before I counted it a lost cause. Unable to cope with my irritability and my personal circumstances, my wife insisted on a divorce. Soon after, she had my car attached. Finally, in total defeat I gathered up my one remaining valuable possession—a flop-eared dog named Franco—and moved in again with my parents. After years of good mental health I was brought to a screeching halt by full-blown episodes of manic-depression. And I had no one to blame but myself!

ﻬ   ﻬ   ﻬ

Struggles of the Caregivers

When someone with strong family ties sinks into worsening episodes of depression, the effect is both disruptive and disheartening for everyone in the unhappy circle. Other family members must now protect the welfare and provide for the needs of their loved one, while at the same time continuing with all their regular duties, responsibilities, and relationships. The added demands upon their time and energies are threatening enough; even worse may be the cloud of embarrassment, anger, blame, resentment, guilt, and confusion under which they must now function.

One immediate difficulty is the possibility of an inaccurate diagnosis. Subject a person classified as depressed to closer scrutiny and he or she may be found to suffer actually from diabetes, Alzheimer's disease (or some other form of dementia), glandular dysfunction, a nutritional deficiency, or an undisclosed addiction. Indeed, medical reference books list approximately seventy-five diseases with early symptoms that include some degree of emotional dysfunction. Accurate diagnosis requires painstaking diligence and well-developed insight in the reading of these symptoms. What appears at first glance to be an emotional problem may later prove a physical dysfunction readily resolved through medical intervention.

Thus it becomes the responsibility of the psychotherapist hearing the complaints of a depressed patient to search with great care for possibilities of biological dysfunction before concluding the problem is merely psychological. To further complicate the process, several different kinds of depression have been identified. A significant number are related to the undersupply or oversupply of certain chemicals which affect our processes of thought and feeling. Even though these chemicals characteristically exist in infinitesimally small amounts, they often fill crucially important roles deep inside the mysterious workings of our brains.

Lacking an accurate diagnosis, family members may be unaware that a chemical imbalance could be the cause of their loved one's bizarre attitude and behavior. They may be too hasty in assigning blame. The limits of love and patience are reached and exceeded. Threats and accusations take the place of courteous exchanges, and before long the struggle against all these unseen foes becomes intense. The result is deterioration in attitudes and relationships. The poison spreads, and family life isn't much fun anymore.

The first strain upon the stability of the family is the increasing absence from ranks of the one who is affected. He or she is no longer dependable, so others must compensate by shouldering new and often unwelcome responsibilities. The severest disruption of family life comes if the patient is the principal wage earner. In this case there is not only the added expense of treatment, but also the inevitable loss of income.

Should the affected person be one of the younger members of the family, the parents suffer the agony of watching their child lose his or her struggle against those personal dragons. And they are dragged unwillingly through the arena, too often as referees. All their hopes and expectations for the child's future seem threatened and may, indeed, need revising. Soon they find themselves in mourning for the achiever who might have been. Instead of a contributor to the family's well-being and image, the affected child may grow up to be a drain upon its energies and finances—an embarrassment, perhaps, and decidedly an emotional liability. This reversal of the family's well-being generates anger and resentment. That, in turn, is reflected in devastating feelings of guilt on the part of all family members unable to cope with the unwelcome circumstances.

Small wonder, then, that loved ones ask, "What is the surest, quickest, and least expensive way to bring him or her out of this and get things back to normal? How can we awaken from this bad dream?" Pain, frustration, and devastating expense threaten cohesiveness and peace within the family unit.

There is also something else—something subtle, but perhaps even more intimidating. The word for it is *stigma*. Too many of us, when someone in a family has what we whisper is a mental problem, place him or her and even the immediate kin under clouds of suspicion. Gossipers see to it no one remains unaware of the dark mysteries within that closet. Former friends and neighbors may cruelly shun the entire family.

That excluding mind-set is only slightly less inhumane than the way the mentally ill were perceived and treated by seventh-century B.C. Phoenicians. A seafaring people, they are said to have corralled their deranged citizens at intervals (and who knows what criteria were used to identify them) and herded them aboard older, less than seaworthy vessels called "ships of fools." Given whatever provisions Phoenician officials saw fit to allow them, they were taken far out into the Mediterranean and set adrift. If they made it on their own to some more hospitable port, well and good. If not . . . ? Since they were considered less than human, their ultimate fate was of no great concern to those who reckoned themselves sane.

Ancient Cures

Through the centuries, various other approaches have been taken in addressing the problem of mental disease. If you lived during the Middle Ages and had the misfortune, fairly or unfairly, to be branded crazy, chances are exorcists would be called in to drive the demons from your deranged head. Other than the influence of wild and uncivilized demons, physicians knew no possible cause for gross unconventional behavior. Each practitioner had his unique way of accomplishing this deliverance from demonic influence, and all were unpleasant. Furthermore, the procedures seldom succeeded.

The idea of an asylum for the insane was developed first in England at the beginning of the fifteenth century. The Hospital of St. Mary of Bethlehem at London's Bishopsgate was converted to that purpose almost five centuries ago, and soon the place became infamous for the brutality shown its mental patients. Inmates deemed in need of restraints were chained to walls, beaten, starved, and treated more cruelly than wild animals. Londoners thought of Bethlehem as a place of chaos and confusion, and its name became a synonym for uproar. Londoners don't pronounce that name *Bethlehem;* in their clipped accent it comes across as *Bedlam.* Many today use that descriptive synonym for chaos without any knowledge of its origin.

The first shock treatments for the mentally ill were introduced at about the same time *Bedlam* was instituted, but electricity hadn't been discovered. The earliest method for attempting to shock the nervous system back to normal was cutting holes in the ice-covered lakes of Europe and dropping patients into the near-freezing water. Now and then, among those who survived the treatment, there were some who showed improvement. Other perhaps more imaginary therapists created rapidly revolving stools and twirled patients until their ears bled. None of the procedures was considered cruel since the patients were deranged. If they managed to survive, it was hoped the kinks would be out of their brains, their rationality restored, and their sanity recovered. What was the success rate? Well, that was before practitioners began keeping reliable research data. The effectiveness of the treatment can only be speculated.

Modern Approach

Today, medical science has contrived more humane tests that provide far more reliable diagnoses. To begin with, the cause and the cure of the disorder can often be identified. In the frequent cases in which a chemical imbalance is causing the symptoms, that imbalance can be brought under control. In our modern culture chains, icy baptisms, and spinning stools are no longer appropriate.

If we have a loved one who suffers severe fits of depression, we instinctively protect him or her from the condemning word *crazy*. We want to know more specifically what is causing the difficulty and what medicine and/or psychological treatment might provide a feasible plan for overcoming it. The question on the lips of thousands who suffer from depression, and thousands more who are their caregivers, is this: *can we ever live normal lives again?*

Medical science's reassuring answer is "Yes, we can help you determine the truth and we can treat the dysfunction." Both blood and urine can be analyzed to determine if an imbalance of lithium or some other chemical might be responsible for serious mood swings threatening the stability of a person's, or a family's, life. Through tireless research and at huge cost, biologists have amassed an impressive amount of knowledge—practical as well as theoretical—concerning both the cause and the cure of depression in its several forms. More knowledge is yet to be gathered, but science already has made an impressive start. Fewer mysteries remain. Researchers are determining authoritative answers to questions like:

- Which brain cells are involved when behavioral changes take place, and exactly what is it that affects them?

- Once the cells are identified, which of the body's chemicals are involved in the changes?

- Why is it these cells suffer imbalance in one person's brain but not in others'?

- Through what tests can this imbalance be verified?

- What glands or tissues are involved in causing the imbalance?

- What medicines in what doses can change the way these organs perform without doing damage to other functions of the body?

Since depression in its various forms first was recognized as a dysfunction, medicine has sought answers to several pragmatic questions. Researchers demand answers that are more reliable than mere theory or starry-eyed optimism:

- Can we treat depression effectively?

- Can we maintain clinical differences between the unipolar and the bipolar?

- Can we cure both, once they are established?

- Can we foresee and prevent them both?

Science of the Mind

Enormous progress has been made in recent years toward a clearer understanding of the functions of the human mind. Indeed, science is making giant steps toward actual interference in these functions to correct them when they go awry. This broadened understanding enables us to review unproven theories rooted in the myths of long ago. From previous generations we have inherited a conceptual gap between the idea of *mind* and the idea of *body*. Findings in recent years have made that gap narrower, but it must be narrowed even more.

Science diligently pursues more than mere knowledge; it aspires not only to understand still unresolved mysteries of body and mind but also to exercise an appropriate degree of control when and where it is needed. In these explorations, science with incredible boldness has probed the secrets of the brain and isolated the very cells from which thought processes emerge. Even the submicroscopic areas between nerve cells and the tissues which link them have been explored, analyzed, and measured. In the process, chemicals synthesized in incredibly small amounts during our thinking and feeling processes are identified and measured. Fewer and fewer of the body's secrets remain undisclosed. Researchers now know the precise building materials from which the walls of brain cells are made. They can identify the very ions that penetrate those walls. These are the chemicals which in proper supply enable us to think and feel.

Having said that, however, we must note on the other side of the coin the sometimes inexact nature of scientific findings. Lamentably, fallibility and ineptitude also are firmly entrenched human frailties even among trained professionals. In spite of incredible scientific advances, we are still confronted by the unsettling fact that today more than one-third of clinical diagnoses of depression prove to be in error. Add to that the number of depressed victims who aren't diagnosed at all, and you sense the frustration of a statistical approach to the problem of mental health.

What we do know is that the behavior of all the body's parts is a consequence of processes originating in the brain. The product—what we do and the way we function, whether voluntarily or involuntarily—is no better than the process which produces it. Thus human behavior springs from a sometimes fickle interaction between the brain's neurons. The possible combinations for even normal interaction between brain cells run into the billions. The process involved is both chemical and electronic, offering an astronomically huge variety of choices in human behavior. But the making of those choices is not a solely mechanical function; it is also voluntary. The process touches upon imbedded values and priorities, and these bring human responsibility into view. Science must not presume it discerns accurately the precise point at which moral responsibility and accountability enter the picture. Still, it must acknowledge that these elusive values are, indeed, part of the process.

Moral Implications

What, then, are the moral, ethical, and ultimately the theological implications of medical research into the workings of the brain? Are we merely biochemical

automatons and thus amoral? Because we call the
function of our brains a process, does it render us no
longer responsible for our choices? Are we merely
the helpless pawns of chemical and cellular interaction in brain matter—a process depending entirely
upon proper function of the machinery? When we
err, can we plead we are victims of chance and elusive combinations beyond our control?

In seeking the answer we should remember that
God's controversy with us apparently has to do primarily with our fallen nature, not with a case by case
documentation of our acts of disobedience and unbelief. The basis for our human dilemma is that we sin
because we are lost, not vice versa. It begins with our
faulty reasonings, especially our reasonings about
God Himself. The grossly irrational applications of
presumptuous faith we find in our society reflect the
reality of that fallen nature.

Who is reponsible, for example, when an Appalachian serpent handler and poison drinker dies in
agony during what he sincerely believes to be a wor-
shipful demonstration of his faith?

Testing Faith with Snakes and Cyanide

On a Saturday night in 1973, in a tiny, one-room
church at the end of a road winding through a little
hollow in Carson Springs, Tennessee, the Cramerton
Mountain Gospel Boys from North Carolina are "making music for Jesus"—lively music—and already the
revelry has begun. Thirty-four-year-old Reverend
Jimmy Ray Williams comes through the door of the
Holiness Church of God in Jesus' Name with his wife,
Mary Kate, and their two children in tow.

Five carloads of friends from North Carolina have made the trip over the mountain with the musicians to sing praises, hear spirit-filled preaching, and see with their own eyes the electrifying performances that set these people apart from less enlightened believers. Men from the visiting group have joined others up front milling around the pulpit while waiting for the preaching to begin. They are taking turns demonstrating the signs and wonders with which a special class of believers in this corner of Appalachia confirm their faith in a miracle-working God. They feel they have discovered His formula for power in an isolated verse at the end of Mark's gospel.

The tools of their worship are unique and frightening, especially to the fainthearted few like Mary Kate. The men hold in their hands not crosses, candles, or incense, but venomous reptiles lifted proudly from boxes behind the pulpit. The paraphernalia of praise used by these rural folk are rattlesnakes, cobras, and water moccasins—reptiles neither defanged nor poison-milked. Enthusiasm runs high as the snakes are fondled and kissed. As quickly as one zealous handler lays down a writhing serpent, another picks it up. As Reverend Robert Grooms will testify later, it is beyond doubt the best meeting he and his brothers and sisters in the Lord have ever witnessed. According to him, "There's lots of anointing!"

Seating his family in the wooden pews, Jimmy Ray strides to the front. Before he picks up one of the snakes he places a vial of legally forbidden strychnine powder on the pulpit. For a moment the cries of "Glory to God!" and "Praise be to Jesus!" are stilled as the worshipers, seeing the vial, realize what may be planned for the climax of tonight's death-defying

praise service. It will be the first time members of
this little church have witnessed someone actually
demonstrating the awesome *fourth* of those five
Spirit-anointed signs.

The Five Signs

> And these signs shall follow them that believe; In
> my name shall they cast out devils; they shall
> speak with new tongues; they shall take up ser-
> pents; and if they drink any deadly thing, it shall
> not hurt them; they shall lay hands on the sick,
> and they shall recover. (Mark 16:17–18, KJV)

In spite of questions that cloud the authenticity of
that particular Bible portion (the oldest and most reliable manuscripts in the original languages close the
chapter with verse eight), snake handlers in the rural
South fervently believe Jesus established these five
signs as a test of faith. They believe that people of
faith are obliged to demonstrate the signs before a
doubting world. Only through these signs can they
confirm the sincerity of their beliefs and testify to the
power of God. Real Christians, they are convinced,
will not only cast out demons and speak in tongues,
they will handle poisonous snakes as well. To complete the list, they should also drink poison and, of
course, heal the sick.

In a little-known book titled *The Persecuted Prophets* (Cranbury NJ: A. S. Barnes & Co., 1976, 85), Robert W. Pelton—apparently, from his writing, a member of the five-signs flock—describes what happened
on that night in Carson Springs when things somehow got out of hand:

The excitement steadily heightened. A great number of people felt the Spirit enter, as was evident in the screams of exuberance accompanied by wild, uninhibited dancing in the pews and aisles. Handclapping and a variety of tongues added to the mood of the moment. The very air seemed charged with a flow of electrical energy. The atmosphere in and around the building was voltaic. There was pure bedlam in the little church.

The Show Goes On

Jimmy Ray now passes his rattlesnake to one of the other men, and with studied deliberateness as the congregation watches transfixed, he pours the strychnine powder into a glass of water, stirring it well. Jimmy Ray displays the instincts of a born showman. For a moment he holds the potion before him as if offering a toast to the Lord. Then he quickly drinks nearly half the poisoned liquid and, without a word, goes back to the box of snakes while Burl Barbee steps up to preach an impassioned sermon about Jesus' power. Pelton's book continues:

> He [Jimmy Ray] was fully enjoying himself in the Holy Ghost. The music seemed to get louder and the crowd reacted accordingly. They stood, jumped, and shouted. Each heightened activity extolled Jesus. They danced wildly and clapped in unison. They raised their arms to the Lord and glorified Him vociferously. (ibid.)

Buford Pack, former paratrooper and father of three children, steps out of the chaos and wraps his hand around the remaining solution of strychnine. Previously, he has demonstrated his faith by drinking battery acid during a tent revival in Brevard,

North Carolina, but this is his first venture with a
deadly poison. Clyde Ricker, who is standing beside
him, testified later that Buford's hand was trembling,
but Clyde insisted it was "the devastating power of
the anointing." Others felt the paratrooper was
frightened.

"I don't know for sure whether this is strychnine
or not," Buford says, "but I'm going to drink it."

"It's strychnine all right," Jimmy Ray says, gri-
macing. By this time he has reason to believe the poison is the real thing.

"I do this to confirm the Word of God," Buford
says solemnly just before he gulps down most of the
remaining liquid. It would have been quicker and
less painful to put a pistol to his temple and pull the
trigger. The book's description continues:

> Whooping, yelling praises to God, and amens
> poured forth from all corners of the church. Buford
> joined his brothers and sisters in the faith as the
> hectic tempo continued as before. . . . He was be-
> coming anointed to preach. He raised his voice no-
> ticeably as he continued above the pandemonium.
> (ibid., 90)

Finishing his sermon, Buford works his way un-
certainly toward the door and goes out into the night
air. Meanwhile, Burl Burbee picks up the glass with a
few swallows left and smells it, hesitating to drink.
Jimmy Ray, still "under the power of a heavy anointing," snatches the poison from him and drains the
glass. Moments later, he falls trembling to the floor.
He is conscious but unable to move his legs.

"Everything will be all right," he gasps as worshipers place him on one of the wooden benches.

Mary Kate hurries to his side, whimpering, terrified, breathing in little gasps.

Don Pack, learning his brother has drunk strychnine, leans against Buford's pink station wagon and peers through the open window to see if his brother is there. "Don't shake the car," an agonized voice mutters from the front seat. Like Jimmy Ray inside the church on the wooden pew, Buford is dying on the seat of his station wagon.

"Lord Jesus, rebuke this poison!" a voice from behind Don commands in prayer.

"God, heal this man!" pleads another.

"Jesus, Jesus, help this brother!"

They were eager to see a miracle—*needed* to see one to fortify their faith.

By this time Buford's face is pale and his lips are blue. Someone massages his arms and legs, and he groans. He has momentary convulsions, but the tremors soon cease and Buford lies still.

Rationalization of Death

Jimmy Ray, barely conscious, is placed in Doyle William's pickup truck and driven down the winding road to his home—his eyes "rolled back and set in his head." Mary Kate rides in another car. In front of the house, still draped across the truck's front seat with Doyle's arm around him, Jimmy Ray grunts his refusal to Sheriff Bobby Stinson's offer to take him to a hospital. Nearly hysterical and unwilling to watch, Mary Kate goes inside with two of the women. Other believers gather around to pray. With voices of authority they cast out demons, loudly demand healing, and call down angels right and left. They are confident the eventful night is about to bring forth a miracle.

Reverend Alfred Ball is less optimistic. He whispers to those nearest this stricken brother in the Lord that a spiritual darkness has descended around him which he believes is an omen from God that Jimmy Ray will die. Still, the men keep on praying. In a few minutes Jimmy Ray goes into violent convulsions. "Hold my legs" he whispers. Thirty seconds later, the tremors cease and he lies still, his eyes open wide. He is no longer breathing.

Buford's limp and lifeless body, draped over the shoulder of his older brother, has already been carried down the road to the Packs' home.

Strangely, this does not contradict the doctrines held by other members of the sect. "They both finished their work," some of the believers explain, nodding their heads and looking to each other for agreement. For a brief moment in history these victims enjoy the status of martyrs. There are no losers. "Yes," says one of the members of the Holiness Church of God in Jesus' Name, "God let them die and go to a better life because He was through with them here on earth. His ways are strange and wonderful."

This is one of the troubling aspects of presumptuous faith. When it falls in disrepute, the actors in the tragic drama can always fabricate an explanation for the doctrinal failure. If their prophecies fail to materialize, they rationalize: "Aha! So that's what He meant! Now we see why God chose to do it a different way." They have God all figured out—*ex post facto*. They presume to think they know His mind. Thus do people making claims through presumptuous faith contribute blithely to their own delinquency.

But, wait—are snake handlers and poison drinkers really appropriate examples of what we term *presumptuous faith?*

Defining *Presumption*

Dictionaries agree *presumption* is the word rightly used when something not convincingly established, however earnestly desired, is *assumed* to be true. One dictionary describes *presumption* as "unwarrantable boldness." Certainly that term applies properly to pointless defiance of death as an act of worship. The God of the Bible gets no glory when those claiming to know Him behave like madmen, and do so in His name. Neither His power nor His wisdom is displayed when His people recklessly and arrogantly handle poisonous snakes, drink lethal poisons, and swallow Drano—all the while "giving glory to God and praise to Jesus."

Another dictionary says *presumption* is "taking something for granted." In a sense that is true, yet there are times when all of us must use well-established premises as presuppositions. For example, those of us who know Christ as Savior "take for granted" certain truths and realities concerning Jesus' person and work. Yet we don't presume Christ's deity, the reality of His ministry on earth, the nature of His miracles, and the efficacy of His death for our sins. We have reliable and authoritative sources for those doctrinal facts. We claim gratefully and without question the forgiveness and acceptance our heavenly Father offers through His grace. As believers we do not question the genuineness of our spiritual birth into His kingdom. All these things are ours through faith based

upon consistent Bible exegesis and final proof lying
in Christ's resurrection from the dead.

Embracing by faith those foundational truths is
not presumptuous. We have solid proof. However,
this confirmation for the foundation of our faith must
flow from the Scriptures and not be contrived by
force and human ingenuity. These truths must be reflected in the historical record, and (more abstractly,
perhaps) in the quiet and rational Word-oriented witness of God the Holy Spirit in the hearts of those
who believe.

Presumptuous, then, seems the proper word for
defining beliefs and supporting rationale *not* supported by Scripture. Doctrines rooted in tradition,
fantasy, or unwarranted emphasis on frivolous detail
can become erroneous and misleading guidelines for
human behavior. Our responsibility as believers is to
determine authoritatively and rationally what is true
and real, and thus what may be taken for granted
concerning God's revealed thoughts and ways. Spurious assumptions and deductions from isolated Bible
texts will not suffice. Neither will confusing *what we
want* with *what God promises* in His Word.

Reckless Deeds for God?

The faith that determines God's will and purpose in
the life of each believer is a tapestry formed not from
a single colored thread but from a blend of the full
spectrum of revealed truth.

Snakes are in the Bible, beginning with the appearance of the serpent in the Garden of Eden when
the devil tempted our first parents to eat the forbidden fruit. The devil is described as both a liar and a

deceiver, and ever since his initial garden appearance he has confused men's minds concerning God. He is "more crafty than any of the wild animals the LORD God had made" (Genesis 3:1), and his most productive work is done in the realm of erroneously conceived religious zeal. Paul reveals that the serpent, the devil himself, still twists people's concept of God:

> But I am afraid that just as Eve was deceived by the serpent's cunning, your minds may somehow be led astray from your sincere and pure devotion to Christ. For if someone comes to you and preaches a Jesus other than the Jesus we preached, or if you receive a different spirit from the one you received, or a different gospel from the one you accepted, you put up with it easily enough. (2 Corinthians 11:3–4)

Paul, of course, had firsthand experience with snakes and the devil. As a prisoner of the Romans shipwrecked on the island of Malta, he gathered a pile of brushwood and built a fire for relief from the rain and cold. Driven out of the brush by the heat of the fire, a deadly viper sank its fangs into the apostle's hand. The superstitious islanders who saw the snake inject poison into this strange visitor assumed he was a murderer being punished by the gods. "The people expected him to swell up or suddenly fall dead, but after waiting a long time and seeing nothing unusual happen to him, they changed their minds and said he was a god" (Acts 28:6).

Three important facts seem plain from that scriptural account:

1. Paul did not deliberately and presumptuously expose himself to the poisonous snake. The ep-

isode was unplanned and unexpected. It was not a demonstration of faith.

2. God in His providence overruled the natural consequences of the snake's venom so Paul could continue the ministry to which he was called.

3. The miraculous event brought no immediate glory to God. Quite the contrary, the natives of Malta decided *Paul himself* was a god and wanted to worship him.

Deeds of reckless daring may bring momentary glory to the person who brandishes venomous snakes or defies natural law by drinking poison, but it is difficult to see how these antics bring glory to God. Perhaps they bring notoriety to the handlers and drinkers, but this hardly glorifies God. The spiritual warfare in which we participate as believers is not between God and the natural processes of His creation; it is between God and invisible principalities and powers of the air. The armament He provides for our defense is not composed of ego-centered weapons of the world (see 2 Corinthians 10:4). God reveals none of His glorious attributes by disarming rattlesnakes and cobras or by making the believer's body immune to self-administered strychnine. The presumptuous process of snake handling and poison drinking is Russian roulette in religious garb. The occasional sacrifice of a life can always be explained by the players; failure does not disprove the thesis but serves only to intensify the pleasure of the hypnotized glory-seekers.

Man's Desire for Power and Control

There is something in all of us that cries out for power—supernatural power that can change the natural order of things. We want to command bad things to go away and see them cower in obedience. We want to be God. We want to claim for ourselves only what is good. We come by that naturally, of course. Lucifer, chief of angels, forfeited his fellowship with God through an attempted assumption of power which could not be his:

> You said in your heart, "I will ascend to heaven; I will raise my throne above the stars of God; I will sit enthroned on the mount of assembly, on the utmost heights of the sacred mountain. I will ascend above the tops of the clouds; I will make myself like the Most High." (Isaiah 14:13–15)

Notice the preponderance of "I's," reflecting an ego that aspires to be "like the Most High." For that effort at self-aggrandizement, Lucifer was cast out of heaven, along with a third of the angels. As the serpent in the Garden of Eden he injected that venom of pride and ambition into the veins of our first ancestors, and the tendency to lust after power has been a human failing ever since.

We are too easily obsessed with a desire to control. For humans, presumption comes quite naturally. We glory in thinking we have discovered a formula which girds us with supernatural power. The death-defying performances of Appalachian snake handlers and poison drinkers is only one of the guises under which that human failing is seen.

Yet these impetuous people are ordinary and sometimes naive folk like lovely Vicki Hoosier from

Micco, West Virginia, who at sixteen regularly handled five-foot rattlesnakes during services in her hometown church. Another was youthful preacher Clyde Ricker of Hot Springs, North Carolina, the first person to handle a lethal Indian cobra and live to tell about it. Also there was Pastor Willie Sizemore of Columbus, Ohio. Regularly in his worship services he filled a Pepsi bottle with kerosene, stuffed a wad of cotton in its neck, struck a match to it, and bathed his face and arms in the eighteen-inch flame. After all, doesn't God promise "the flames will not set you ablaze" (Isaiah 43:2)? His parishioners insist Willie wasn't burned.

Then there was Floyd McCall, a muscular believer from Greenville, South Carolina, who, when properly "anointed," gulped down battery acid or ate handfuls of Drano "to show that God's Word is true." And lastly, there was the venerable Bishop Kelly Williams of Switzer, West Virginia, reported to have drunk gallons of strychnine over a quarter-century without suffering as much as a stomachache.

Not all of them succeeded, however. Richard Lee Williams of Hilliard, Ohio, was one of this unique company until a fateful evening on 2 April 1974. He conducted revival services in the Full Gospel Jesus Church in Kistler, West Virginia, where believers gleefully handle poisonous snakes. A giant diamondback rattler bit Brother Williams in the palm of his left hand, then sank its fangs into an artery in his wrist. Doctors who treat snakebite victims estimate rattlesnakes kill only 1 percent of the people they bite, but Richard Lee was to come up on the short side of those statistics.

With a handkerchief wrapped around his wrist to staunch the bleeding, the handsome young preacher spoke for a while to an anxious congregation, assuring them he would be all right. Urging the saints to pray for him, he then went to a nearby home where he was staying for what had been planned as a week of soul winning.

By the next morning Richard Lee was in agony and his arm had swelled to a grotesque size and shape. The skin on the inside of his elbow had burst and the wound was draining. Bravely, he refused to call a doctor, saying God would heal him. He was conscious almost to the end. At three o'clock in the afternoon Richard Lee took his last breath. Incredibly, his colleagues saw it as victory, not defeat. Concerning that senseless tragedy, author Pelton writes this fanciful benediction:

> He was hammered to the cross on Calvary's hill. Richard Williams had a short but effective and far-reaching ministry. He was an evangelist, a teacher, and a diligent worker in the signs. His faith gave him a new life. He has given his life for that faith. (ibid., 163)

Others, however, might experience difficulty accepting the pointless death of a bright and handsome young evangelist as anything other than a repugnant exercise in presumptuous faith.

4

WHO NEEDS THIS MESSIAH?

I was in the psychiatric ward for only seven days—a week that began a drastic and frightening change in my life.

Each morning I awoke to find a different religious tract beside my pillow. I couldn't figure out where these messages were coming from. My reaction went first to resentment, then mild curiosity, and finally lively interest. These were messages about Christ, and all of them came from something or somebody called *Jews for Jesus* and *Voice* magazine.

I had a personal problem with that. The Jews I grew up with didn't give much thought to Jesus. Not that they were against Him; they just weren't *for* Him. So *Jews for Jesus* seemed a strange contradiction of terms. Within three days, though, I found myself looking forward to reading what these unconventional people had to say about Jesus—the controversial man some of our Jewish forefathers identified as their long-awaited *Mashiach*. But why me? What kind of person thought it important that I learn all this stuff about Jesus. Was it possible I'd been missing something all these years? I was eager to know *who* was leaving those tracts beside my pillow and why I was the target.

Some of the messages were worded diplomatically; others were blunt and hard hitting. All of them were about Jesus, who was always presented as our Jewish *Mashiach*. I thought it curious that this wasn't just New Testament stuff; a lot of the statements about Jesus were taken from the Jewish Bible—what Old Testament prophets had written. It sounded as if there might be a connection. What if He really was the Messiah?

I'll level with you: what seemed especially disturbing was that the tracts referred to heaven and hell as if they were real places—places to which people like me actually go after they die. Since my qualifications didn't seem to fit me for heaven, it wasn't hard to figure what the alternative would be. What I couldn't understand was what Jesus had to do with all that. The tracts seemed to be saying, "It's your eternity, so take your pick, but examine all the evidence before you choose." That was unsettling—so unsettling that I wanted to read more.

Like everyone else, I had thought about God now and then. I had wondered about who and where and *if* He is and what He might be like. It hadn't occurred to me, though, to think about pleasing Him or wonder if I'd be with Him after I died. After I read a couple of those mystery messages things began to change. I couldn't think of much else. Those questions about God were on my mind most of the time.

"Did you get the tracts I left?" a doctor friend asked one day toward the end of my week. He wasn't my psychiatrist; he was the father of my best friend. I had idolized him when I was a child. He dropped in regularly just to say hello, usually after his early morning rounds.

"You left me all that stuff about Jesus?" I blurted out. A fellow *Jew* putting stuff about Christ under my pillow?

"Sure," and something about his gentle smile got to me. "You read 'em, huh?"

"Well, yeah," I replied, as casually as possible.

"Good," he said nonchalantly. Then, "Well, I've got to make some more rounds. If you need anything, Stan, let me know."

"Yeah, fine," I said, because I couldn't think of anything else.

Then, turning as he reached the door, he really blew my mind. He said "God bless you, Stan. I love you and I'll be praying for you."

Then, before I could think of something to say he was out the door and on his way down the hall.

Love me? I didn't know normal people talked like that.

My doctor friend had me on the ropes. I spent the rest of the day wondering, *What's this love stuff, and this stuff about the Messiah? And what's it all got to do with my mixed-up life?*

The next day I was released from the hospital and went home clutching my bottle of medicine. I also bundled up the *Jews for Jesus* tracts and took them along, just in case I decided to read them again.

I'd resigned myself to the lithium carbonate pills, but I had come to depend on Valium more than anyone knew—dependent enough to get me in trouble. Three months later, my pharmacist confronted me about my excess use of Valium. When I lied to cover up, he called all of my doctors to relay his suspicion that I was abusing the mood-altering drug. He refused to be responsible for filling my Valium prescription again. So all of a sudden, cold turkey—I had to do without my emotional crutch. I begged for some medicine to replace the Valium, but the psychiatrist held his ground.

"Don't worry about it; you'll live," he assured me. "The lithium's enough." And live I did, finally winning the battle. I don't know why God would be interested in helping me, but I think He did. I lost thirty-five pounds in the process and began to fear I had a terminal illness, but somehow I completed my withdrawal from habit-forming drugs.

About that time I learned my doctor friend hadn't given up on the Messiah business. He invited me to go with him to a breakfast—an event he thought I'd find interesting.

"What kind of breakfast?" I asked, getting strong signals that I was about to get a religious hustling.

"Oh, you might say it's religious," he responded. "If you need a name, we call the group the FGBMFI."

"Which means . . . ?" I pressed.

"The Full Gospel Business Men's Fellowship International," he recited.

It sounded ominous. "Why me?" I wanted to know.

"Because you've begun something that ought to be finished," he replied. "A lot of eternal business gets finished at these breakfasts."

I wasn't aware of any unfinished business, but I was always one to accept a challenge. I was also curious about this Messiah bit, so I agreed to let my doctor friend buy my breakfast, resolving to be on guard against unwelcome religious propaganda. A few days later I found myself eating scrambled eggs and sausage with the FGBMFI, an enthusiastic and demonstrative bunch of guys on a Jesus kick. They praised the Lord, recited Bible verses, and waved their arms a lot. One of them prayed in a strange, repetitious language I couldn't identify. Before that breakfast meeting I'd never heard of the organization, but it turned out these men had heard of me. My doctor friend had them praying for me—a fact which caused me mixed emotions.

In a way, I was touched; on the other hand, I resented their meddling in my life. For some strange reason I felt intimidated by these men. Maybe they were a bit spacey, and even more, naive, but there was something *good* about them. They spoke of God as if He was someone people can get to know personally, and I knew I'd never bothered to get acquainted.

Before we ate, some of them took turns sitting in a special chair to receive prayer, and the next thing I knew they were urging me to take my turn. Not wanting to hurt their feelings by declining, I found myself sitting there praying a sinner's prayer one of the men recited for me. I didn't mean what I said, and I had a feeling they weren't fooled by my performance, but I parrotted the words. Not surprisingly, nothing happened—not inside, not outside. The man who prayed with me—not a businessman but a pastor, it turned out—volunteered to drive me home, and he told me all the things I must do or not do now that I had "accepted the Lord." At the top of his list was sex. No more "lust of the flesh" for Stan Schmidt.

That not-very-subtle invasion of my privacy set-tled my last doubts; I had definitely gotten myself involved with the wrong crowd. The well-inten-tioned pastor presented me with his telephone num-ber and a book called *Come and Live*, by Tom C. McKenney, but I didn't call him, and I threw his book under my bed.

I also called my doctor friend the next day and instructed him not to invite me to any more breakfast meetings. I wouldn't be going. I tried to be nice about it, but I had to be firm.

"Okay," he said. "I love you, Stan, and I'll be praying for you."

There it was again. He loved me—whatever that meant. To tell the truth, my initial reaction to that was a two-syllable synonym for barnyard droppings. People don't go around loving each other that way, especially not men. I'd seen too much of life's dark side to believe that pipe dream. I thought, *These breakfast-prayer-meeting guys don't know when to quit!*

Deep down inside, though, I found myself hoping my doctor friend would not.

ð«   ð«   ð«

Reclassifying the Disease

Dr. Frank Bolea, who wrote the foreword to this book, thinks manic-depression should be rediscov-ered and reclassified. He hopes medical science soon will rethink the disorder's definitions. In a letter to the authors he writes:

We need to start over again and see the subject from a new and different angle. Therapeutic approach to bipolar affective disorders too often is with an emphasis on psychology or psychiatry. We know now that these particular disorders are basically physical instead of mental, so when we put together our statistics on manic-depression we probably ought to move them from the mental column to the physical column.

Because the problem affects the brain, psychotherapy is rightly involved in the treatment, but at the root of all the trouble is usually a chemical imbalance. "From now on," Dr. Bolea asserts, "I expect the most productive research in affective disorders will be in the field of biochemistry and physiotherapy, not in the realm of psychotherapy."

Dr. Bolea reminds us that, technically, *curable* cannot be properly applied to most illnesses. "A very high percentage of medical interventions are designed to remove pain and discomfort and prevent further damage," he points out. Diabetes and the use of insulin is a prime example. Obvious exceptions are infections and surgically treatable cases, but high on the list of medical priorities is the treatment of symptoms and the avoidance of further complications—in reality, still delaying the inevitable. Dr. Bolea's letter continues:

Lithium does not *cure* manic-depression. It is the most effective way to *control* it. Though the cause of this disorder remains a mystery, we know that lithium can bring a person out of a state of mania and return him to a normal state, and it can help prevent episodes of mania and depression from recurring. The fact that this is a process of *controlling*

rather than of *curing* the disorder means that
should patients stop taking their lithium, manic or
depressive episodes would likely recur.

Postponing the End

Medical practitioners aspire primarily to improve the
quality or prolong the quantity of life for a stricken
patient, and when they accomplish that, their work is
usually considered successful. Physicians and patients alike understand that our bodies are not permanent fixtures on earth. In the long run when we
intervene with medicine—often even with surgery—
we only postpone the end. The concept of *illness* on
one side of the ledger and *cure* on the other may be
unique to modern Western civilization. Great forward strides made by medical science help encourage that sometimes misleading concept. Even when
Jesus miraculously dealt with diseases, lameness,
blindness, and deafness, the benefits were temporary.
Sooner or later, those He healed would face the final
enemy: death. He brought Lazarus out of the tomb
after his body was lifeless for three days (see John
11), but the miraculous deliverance was not a cure; it
was a postponement. Lazarus eventually was gathered to his ancestors in the family tomb.

Not all human ills are caused by germs, accident,
abuse of the body, or environmental circumstances.
Many of our physical problems are rooted in defects
in the genetic package we receive at conception.
There is strong clinical evidence from twin, family,
and adoption studies that hereditary factors play a
significant role in some cases of manic-depression.
Close relatives of someone with the disorder are

more likely to develop symptoms than those not related. Still, such findings are far from decisive. Where manic-depression is diagnosed, hereditary factors are not always apparent. As a result, it is not possible to accurately predict the risk factor for those related to someone suffering from the disorder.

We are all flawed products of a flawed universe. Even when these defects are treated successfully with medicines, they may not properly be called cured. It is more realistic to think of them as abated. If the patient ceases or neglects his medication, the symptoms will likely return. That is why no matter how sincere or intense the afflicted person's faith, he or she should continue taking the medicine, at least until the anticipated miracle is unmistakably confirmed.

Surveys indicate that a surprising number of psychiatric patients consider their problem the result of a fault-and-punishment cycle, divine or otherwise. Guilt plays a significant part in that perception, and guilt can also exacerbate the symptoms. When symptoms subside, many patients perceive the improvement as miraculous deliverance and thus are tempted to forego the medicine that likely caused the improvement. Others may see it as just plain luck, the magic of modern medicines, a reflection of the doctor's rare skills, or the intercession of someone who "really knows how to pray." Few seem able to recognize the so-called mental problem as a natural but correctable result of our human frailty and genetic package.

When the symptoms subside under treatment, that also is a natural consequence. Responsible faith frequently plays a part in the healing process, but that does not rule out the use of God-given chemicals to replace those apparently lacking in the neurotransmitters of the afflicted person's brain cells.

Use of Lithium

In 1970, the Food and Drug Administration approved the use of lithium as an effective means of controlling bipolar affective disorders. A simple, natural chemical found in certain rock formations, lithium tends to stabilize the disabling elation-to-despair mood swings which characterize victims of manic-depression.

Because its side effects are generally fewer and less severe than those resulting from other medicines, lithium now is the preferred treatment for bipolar affective disorders. A few people feel better as soon as they start taking lithium, but most experience the benefits more gradually. Some may have to wait several weeks before noticeable improvement begins. Thus it is important that the patient who goes on this medication stay with the regimen. As often as not, "stay" means the rest of his life. The "aspirin" mindset has proved costly for many: "I took the medicine and it cured me, so I don't have to take it any more." Lithium does not cure; it controls.

Since the chemical's use is complicated, not all physicians are trained to prescribe lithium in proper doses. Therapists lacking medical degrees do not prescribe it at all. The patient for whom the use of lithium has been indicated will find more complete information in *Lithium and Manic Depression: A Guide* (Madison, WI: Lithium Information Center, 1988).

Most patients taking lithium experience few if any side effects from the medication. It is not addictive. There is evidence that lithium, taken for long

periods or in high doses, may, in a small number of
people, cause permanent damage to kidney tissue.
This is rare, but the danger makes a periodic testing
of kidney function a prudent part of lithium therapy.
Lithium may also cause the thyroid gland to enlarge
or become underactive. This is treated with relative
ease, however, by taking supplementary thyroid
medication.

Some patients may experience other minor difficulties, though these usually reflect the body's initial response to the chemical and likely will disappear in a
few weeks. For example, the patient may feel slightly
nauseated and have mild stomach cramps. He or she
may be drowsy or dizzy at times. There may be de-
creased sexual interest or ability. The mouth may be
dry and the patient may experience a metallic taste.
All of these symptoms are usually temporary. Other
side effects have been known to persist, like increased
thirst and urination, weight gain, and tremor of the
hands. Most physicians who prescribe lithium will
caution the patient to report promptly any side effects
severe enough to be threatening.

Our body's circulatory system is the mechanism
that transports that lithium—along with other chemicals, nutrients, oxygen, and hormones—to the brain
and to the body's other organs and tissues. As our
blood circulates it also collects and carries away
much of the body's waste, distributing oxygen as it
travels in arteries from lungs to organs, and gathering carbon dioxide for its return trip via the veins. In
explaining the rationale for blood sacrifice in Old
Testament liturgies, Moses wrote, "For the life of a
creature is in the blood" (Leviticus 17:11). Modern

medicine made that discovery less than a century and a half ago!

The average adult body contains approximately ten pints of blood, and when the body is at rest the entire volume circulates through it every minute. During strenuous exercise, the blood can be pumped four times as fast. Our circulatory system is an incredibly complicated mechanism which adjusts constantly to changes in the body's demands. Small wonder there are times when our brains seem less nimble than usual!

It is largely through controlling body chemistry and replacing blood when the supply is depleted that medical science can contribute significantly to our well-being. When the chemistry cannot be analyzed or replacement blood is not available or denied, medical science often finds its hands tied.

Watchtower Society

Winifred Melton (not her real name) became just another hospital statistic when she spurned a blood transfusion. According to hospital records, she was "confused and barely conscious" when time began to run out. As orderlies transferred her to the coronary care unit, her heart was slowly dying for lack of blood. The tragedy—the factor frustrating the hospital's medical staff to the point of outrage—was that it didn't have to be that way. Winifred's story is a sad mismatch between presumptuous faith and human frailty.

The wife and mother of two teenagers was only forty-two when she first reported to her family physician a small amount of blood in her urine—a common complaint from women prone to bladder infections. Antibiotics usually alleviate the symptoms. In Winifred's case, however, the doses seemed to make things worse.

A urologist's fiber-optic scope then located and removed the real cause—a small tumor attached to the bladder's inner wall. Since such tumors tend to recur, Winifred was told to report promptly any similar symptoms. For several years she had repeated episodes of bleeding, always cared for promptly by her urologist. Iron supplements handily replaced the red blood cells she had lost. It was a minor inconvenience, but far from life-threatening. Then Winifred grew careless.

With her last tumor she delayed her visit to the doctor until she was bleeding profusely and already was severely anemic. Before the surgery could be performed, doctors decided she must have a blood transfusion. All was routine until the patient refused. No amount of reasoning or explanations of the threat to her life could change her mind. Blood transfusions were displeasing to God and against her religion. Winifred was a Jehovah's Witness.

From that point things for Winifred went steadily downhill. Nothing the surgeons tried could staunch the bleeding. Her blood count dropped lower and lower until finally she was no longer a viable candidate for surgical repairs. "You must understand our helplessness," her doctors warned her. "Without a blood transfusion you will die." She was an intelligent woman; she understood the implications. But Winifred stuck by her priorities. Die or not, she would be loyal to her faith. God had banned such use of blood, the symbol of life itself.

In the August 1988 edition of *Discover* magazine, Dr. Elisabeth Rosenthal describes Winifred's final moments:

> At the center of everyone's attention was a large woman with an oxygen mask, gasping for air, breathing faster than seemed humanly possible. At the head of the bed were three friends, fellow church members, coaching her through her moment of wretched glory.
>
> "Your friend is going to die," I told them. "I will take her up to the coronary care unit because I legally have to, but there will be nothing effective I can do. We will give her oxygen, but her blood is already carrying all the oxygen it can hold."
>
> They listened patiently, wincing as I described some of the more ghoulish aspects of the night to come.
>
> They clearly understood my point. But this is not (for them) a rational matter. "I'm sorry this is going to be a lot of trouble for you," one of them said. "It may not make any sense to you, but she does understand that she might die."
>
> And die she did, a very short time later, but only after the full charade of Epinephrine, Atropine, shock, CPR, a weary medical crew and a bed littered with EKG tracings, syringe tops, and blood. Given a transfusion to replace the blood she had lost, the wife and mother could have lived. Without it, she didn't have a chance.
>
> "This doesn't make sense to you, we know," apologized one of Winifred's friends. "You see, we believe . . ." and she pulled a copy of *Watchtower* from her purse.

No one will ever know how many Jehovah's Witnesses have died needlessly during or following surgery because they adamantly refused the blood transfusion that would have spared their lives. Such statistics are not gathered by the Watchtower Society and would not be released by their Governing Body if they were. Neither is there any record of the number of children of Jehovah's Witnesses who have died of leukemia or diabetic complications or from trauma following an accident, helplessly trusting their parents' judgment not to allow the medical treatment that could save them.

Faithful unto Death

Such faith comes in many forms. Each year, nearly a quarter of a million new Watchtower Society recruits join nine million others around the globe already submitting themselves to the stern laws and the mailed fist of the Governing Body. Estranged from society by fear of Jehovah God's judgment and their radical separationist doctrines, Jehovah's Witnesses stoically embrace death itself rather than allow blood transfusions for themselves or their loved ones. Neither do they salute the flag, serve in the armed forces, vote in elections, celebrate birthdays, observe Christmas and Easter, or attend the church of another denomination. Rationale for that lengthy list of don'ts follows two lines of reasoning:

1. All government and all "religion" (other than Jehovah's Witnesses) is under the power of Satan. The real people of God, then, must not involve themselves with His enemies—not at any level of government or in dealings with any aspect of false religions.

2. Blood is sacred to man and to God. The Bible commands believers to "abstain" from blood (not to eat animals improperly bled). A transfusion is just as serious a violation of that binding law as the drinking of blood.

The Truth that Leads to Eternal Life, a Watchtower Society publication which boasts more than one hundred million copies in print in 115 languages, quotes third-century theologian Quintus Tertullian to make its case against blood transfusions:

> Those, too, who at the gladiator shows, for the cure of epilepsy, quaff with greedy thirst the blood of criminals slain in the arena, as it flows fresh from the wound, and then rush off—to whom do they belong? Blush for your vile ways before the Christians, who have not even the blood of animals at their meals of simple and natural foods; who abstain from things strangled and that die a natural death. (p. 167)

We identify readily with Tertullian's revulsion at the thought of epileptic Romans rushing into arenas to drink the still-warm blood of executed criminals. That makes a less than convincing case, however, against blood transfusions as a legitimate medical procedure in the saving of a life. Besides, like the edicts of the Watchtower Society's Governing Body itself, Tertullian's writings lack the authority of the Word of God.

Life in the Blood

The finally understood medical fact that the body's life depends upon its blood supply doubtless provides the basis for God's warning. Likely other factors in God's reasoning relate to the health of the one who eats a blood product. For whatever reasons He warns, "Any Israelite or any alien living among them who eats any blood—I will set my face against that person who eats blood and will cut him off from his people" (Leviticus 17:10).

How did that work? The ancient Jewish hunter who went into the woods with bow and arrow and killed, say, an antelope, had to take care to drain the animal's blood and cover it with dirt. Otherwise the meat was considered unclean and could not be eaten. No doubt valid health and dietary reasons can be found for that rule, but there were also ceremonial reasons. Blood sacrifices were prototypes foreshadowing the substitutionary death of Jesus Christ for our sins. But Tertullian, and perhaps the Jehovah's Witnesses as well, appears to have overlooked Paul's explicit warning to the young and wayward church at Colossae:

> Therefore do not let anyone judge you by what you eat or drink, or with regard to a religious festival, a New Moon celebration or a Sabbath day. These are a shadow of the things that were to come; the reality, however, is found in Christ. . . .
>
> Since you died with Christ to the basic principles of this world, why, as though you still belonged to it, do you submit to its rules: "Do not handle! Do not taste! Do not touch!" These are all destined to perish with use, because they are based on human commands and teachings. Such regulations indeed have an appearance of wisdom, with their self-imposed worship, their false humility and their harsh treatment of the body, but they lack any value in restraining sensual indulgence. (Colossians 2:16–17, 20–23)

Abstaining from Blood

Tertullian's writings profoundly influenced Christianity in his day, but his rigorous ascetic agenda and his often harsh and sarcastic criticism of those who did not conform to his views raised serious questions concerning the authority of his opinions. He held that Christians should welcome persecution, not flee from it. Jehovah's Witnesses are in solid agreement on that score. Tertullian argued that only the church has the authority to declare which beliefs are orthodox and which are not, leaving ample room for presumptuous demands upon loyal adherents. Ditto the Watchtower Society's Governing Body. Tertullian also staunchly defended the ecclesiastical right to dictate the behavior and control the lives of believers. Jehovah's Witnesses gladly, at least on the surface, submit to that absolute control. Small wonder the monolithic Watchtower Society leadership quotes from Tertullian's writings to support the presumptuous beliefs it demands from its members. Those who resist are subject to a disfellowshipping process which leaves them shunned and rejected even by their family members.

Jehovah's Witnesses insist the Old Testament proscription against blood is imposed upon New Testament Christians through a letter from the Jerusalem assembly providing guidelines for Gentile believers in Antioch, Syria, and Cilicia: "You are to abstain from food sacrificed to idols, from blood, from the meat of strangled animals and from sexual immorality. You will do well to avoid these things. Farewell" (Acts 15:29).

Inexplicably, however, the Watchtower Society's *New World Translation of the Holy Scriptures* gives that verse a significantly different meaning. The differences are italicized: "Keep yourselves free from things sacrificed to idols and from blood and from things strangled and from fornication. If you carefully keep yourselves from these things, *you will prosper. Good health to you!*"

Note the addition by the Watchtower translators of a promise of prosperity and a promise of good health to those who follow the Old Testament dietary laws. No other contemporary translation takes such liberty with the text. Promises of prosperity and health simply do not appear in Luke's Greek. *The Truth that Leads to Eternal Life* insists "abstaining from blood" means not taking it into our bodies at all, not even by transfusion to save a life.

Accepting the Risk

Most Jehovah's Witnesses carry signed cards saying "I direct that no blood transfusions be given to me, even though physicians deem such vital to my health or my life. . . . I accept the added risk this may bring. I release doctors, anesthesiologists, hospitals and their personnel from responsibility for any untoward results caused by my refusal, despite their competent care." Small wonder emergency room teams groan when they find such a card on a bleeding accident victim!

Many emergency room physicians, however, say their Hippocratic oath compels them to administer blood just the same, since they have no way of knowing if the card accurately reflects a patient's beliefs under the desperate circumstances in which they may be treating him. "In general, if the patient clearly needed blood or would die, most physicians are going to give blood," said one emergency room doctor who spoke on condition he not be identified. He explained his desire for anonymity by saying, "It's a no-win situation. If I say we give blood no matter what, then the Jehovah's Witnesses will be after us. If I say we don't give blood, then the right-to-lifers will be up in arms. I've heard of cases in which the patient and the family said 'no blood,' the patient died, and the family sued, saying if they had known the situation was that bad they would have authorized a transfusion."

At Brookhaven Memorial Hospital in East Patchogue, New York, three Jehovah's Witnesses were arrested in January 1989 when they tried to prevent a critically ill church member from receiving a blood transfusion ordered by hospital authorities. The patient was hemorrhaging after a Caesarean section delivery, and attendants considered her life gravely at risk.

Police were called to the hospital when fifteen people, including the woman's husband, surrounded her bed and refused to allow the transfusion for which the hospital had obtained a court order. The woman's husband and two other Jehovah's Witnesses were arrested on charges of criminal trespassing.

A lawsuit may be pending. Adamant Jehovah's Witnesses say they would file suit against anyone who gives Watchtower Society members blood, accusing the medical team of committing assault and battery by violating their wishes. Still, if blood is forced upon an unwilling Jehovah's Witness while he is unconscious or because of a court order, the organization's authorities agree there are no punitive theological consequences for the violated member. God understands the circumstances, they concede, and does not hold the victim responsible.

Does the proscription against life-giving blood place Watchtower Society members at a disadvantage in terms of their health? They don't think so. They argue that in prohibiting the ingestion of blood God includes the promise of prosperity and good health for a specific purpose. "He knows what he is talking about!" *The Truth that Leads to Eternal Life* comments. To them, the promise carries the Jehovah's Witnesses' case from the negative to the positive. To these people, thanks to that promise of prosperity and good health, the advantage goes to those who *refuse* a blood transfusion. They have God on the side of their physical well-being. "The fact is," their little blue book says, "that while most patients survive blood transfusions, many become diseased as a result of them and thousands die every year as a direct result of them." Medical statistics fail to confirm that observation, even with the onset of the AIDS epidemic.

The crucial question, however, is whether or not Acts 15:29 actually holds forth that promise of prosperity and health. The Modern Language Bible renders the verse's closing sentences, "If you keep yourselves clear from these, you will get along splendidly. Farewell." No mention is made of health or prosperity there either. Even the sometimes loosely worded Living Bible says only, "If you do this, it is enough. Farewell." No reference to any physical advantage for those untainted by blood appears in the original language. Only the Jehovah's Witness translators presume to add it, yet to these diligent and obedient men and women it has become the unyielding law of God.

Curiously, the chapter in *The Truth that Leads to Eternal Life* titled "Godly Respect for Life and Blood" ends with "He sent his Son Jesus Christ to shed his own lifeblood on behalf of those who will exercise faith. . . . only by means of faith in Jesus' shed blood can salvation be had." Bible believers wholeheartedly agree with that. The statement is an accurate summarization of God's redemptive plan, but that doctrine does not appear to be what Jehovah's Witnesses really believe. Like the Pharisees of old, their presumptuous faith places them under bondage to obey the edicts of their Governing Body. Failure to comply in every detail means being disfellowshipped, shunned, cut off from family and friends, and—probably holding them in bondage even more firmly than the other threats—banished from the presence of Jehovah God for all eternity.

"Better to submit, even to die, than break God's law and miss out on eternal life," Jehovah's Witnesses say as they close their case for presumptuous faith.

5

CHANGES FOR THE BETTER

*R*ebirth *doesn't have to be a religious experience,* I thought. *I'll accomplish the same thing by changing my ways—partying less and improving the old brain.*

On my first trip to the public library the eerie quietness enabled me to turn to deeper matters. There among other silent figures huddled over books, papers, and magazines—and one or two taking naps on the sly—I began thinking seriously about God. I reflected on the difference between what is and what ought to be in my life. Something told me I wasn't doing very well. So I decided to begin unraveling those tangled threads.

I hadn't read a book for years, so the simple act of going to the library was a radical move. It seemed a good place to begin a different life-style. With that first step in a new direction I was off and running on a determined program to straighten up my life.

High on my agenda was saying good-bye to drugs, druggies, and drug dealers. That senseless and expensive recreation was getting me nowhere fast. By God's grace I managed to get that troublesome monkey off my back.

Rid of that excess baggage, I began to enjoy life for a change. Here I was, former life of the party and proud star of the athletic field metamorphosed into a library freak whose most exciting indulgence was a long walk in the woods, a good movie, or twenty laps in a public swimming pool! I found myself wondering who this new Stan Schmidt was, and what mystical force had brought about the change.

Mystical force? Could it have anything to do with the prayers of my doctor friend? Or, maybe his strange associates at the FGBMFI were behind it—those guys who took their religion so seriously. It couldn't have been that prayer chair, could it? I sat in that thing for the wrong reasons, but it was true I mouthed the words of their sinner's prayer. Tongue in cheek, I asked Jesus, repeating the dictated formula, to take over my life.

If Jesus wasn't the force behind all this, who was?

In the library on June 6, 1986, I determined to get some answers. I took advantage of the quietness and did some heavy praying. Always a bit dubious about other people's religious formulas, I worded my own prayer this time. I asked God to please reach down and do for me whatever I needed most. That needn't be money or health or anything else tangible; perhaps it was just plain peace of mind. Above all, I needed to know the truth. Who *is* this Jesus? I wanted to settle those nagging doubts about God. Maybe I could even settle the matter of who *I* was. I wanted to know what God required of me and what I could do about it. I thought, *Maybe a Bible will help.* Finding a Bible on the library's shelves, I began thumbing through it and immediately wondered, *Where do I start?*

The Gospel of John sounded familiar, so I looked it up in the table of contents and began to read about the Word made flesh, about Jesus coming to His Jewish people who didn't receive Him. Yet to anyone who did—and some who received Him were Jews like me—He gave the authority to be children of God. Does that mean those who *don't* receive Him *aren't* children of God? I certainly hadn't received Him yet.

I learned from John's Gospel about a Jewish authority who wanted to talk with Jesus about God. Jesus surprised him with the statement that without a spiritual rebirth people can't enter the kingdom of heaven, implying, I suppose, that just talking about God is a futile exercise. Then He made the startling claim that spiritual rebirth comes only through knowing *Him!* But how does someone go about getting acquainted with Jesus when He walked the earth two thousand years ago? Still, wasn't that business about spiritual rebirth what my Jewish doctor friend and his FGBMFI buddies were saying?

Then I thought of the book the stern pastor gave me—the book inviting readers to *Come and Live.* If I remembered correctly, that little volume was last seen as it disappeared under my bed. Would *Come and Live* help me understand this stuff? I hurried home to find out.

When I retrieved the book from under my bed, there was the rebirth stuff again. Chapter six was titled, "Ye Must be Born Again"—the same thing Jesus said to the Jewish leader named Nicodemus!

Maybe this sounds too dramatic to be real and even a bit corny, but I decided it was time I stopped dodging reality. The end of that chapter found me on my knees beside my bed. All of a sudden I knew just being religious was out and really believing the truth about God was in. Somebody had to suffer the consequences of my sin, and apparently it had to be either me or Jesus. There's no divine test of character. I don't have to master mystical formulas or perform acts of heroic sacrifice. God just wants my trust, and the right place to get started was on my knees. The promise is to "whosoever believes in him," and believing is something even I can do. So I prayed that sinner's prayer again, as best I could remember it and in my own words, just to be sure. I held a private coronation ceremony, and by faith I crowned Jesus my *Mashiach* and my Lord. I felt wonder and gratitude as I considered my long, tough struggle. It was like getting home again after a long and frightening journey. At that moment I know I was born into God's Kingdom.

Next, I did what you probably would do in the same circumstances: I called my Jewish Christian friend and thanked him for loving me and praying for me. I told him I thought I'd finally learned what he meant when he said he loved me. I asked him to thank his friends and the pastor who gave me the book.

"Thank them yourself," he said. "Our next breakfast is tomorrow morning. I'll pick you up at six fifteen."

I wasn't altogether awake, but the men seemed genuinely glad to see me. After I reported what I'd discovered at long last about Jesus, they were downright jubilant. Most of them promised to keep on praying for me.

One of the men, however, seemed a little grim. He pulled me aside and asked, "Stan, have you considered the possibility that demons are causing your bipolar illness?"

"Demons?" I said.

"Demons," he repeated. "Illnesses, particularly illnesses of the mind, are directly related to the spirit world. The demons only yield to our claims of faith when we use the spiritual power Jesus gives us."

"You mean some kind of . . . uh, invisible spirit might be causing my mood swings," I asked in wonder.

"That's what I mean," he replied. "I feel you ought to claim your deliverance and let God give you the victory. It seems to me taking medicine is a denial of God's power to heal us."

"I'll think about it," I said, and I suspect he knew I was waffling. I wasn't ready yet for demons. Besides, my lithium carbonate pills were working fine.

I didn't follow up on the demon business, but it wasn't long before I was listening with mounting interest to talk about faith healing. I found a charismatic church and went through various supernatural experiences.

Then came the question destined to bring me crashing down. "Stan," my pastor said to me one day, pulling me aside where we could talk privately, "do you have enough faith to throw away those lithium pills?"

"You mean, get off my medicine?" I asked.

"That's what I mean," he said, and he seemed to see right past the doubts and fears his question generated. "If you've got enough faith, Jesus will heal you. It's in the atonement." Then he quoted the Old Testament verse I'd be hearing again and again in charismatic circles: "But he was pierced for our transgressions, he was crushed for our iniquities; the punishment that brought us peace was upon him, and *by his wounds we are healed"* (Isaiah 53:5, emphasis added).

"By His wounds we are *healed*," he said, bearing down on the word. "God doesn't want us lost, and He doesn't want us sick, either. He took care of us inside and out when Jesus hung on that cross. When Spirit-filled Christians are sick, it's the devil's lie. Why don't you just claim your deliverance and get rid of those pills once and for all?" So *that's* what Isaiah meant when he wrote "By his wounds we are healed"!

How was I to know that passage has been debated for centuries by well-meaning spokesmen from various theological camps? Healed! To me it seemed incredible enough that my spiritual healing took place when Jesus died in my place. I thought that's what the Messiah was supposed to do for us. But to a manic-depressive, physical and mental healing sounded even greater. Because I was in the faith it never occurred to me to get a second opinion.

My pastor considered my bipolar disease a clear-cut attack by the devil himself, and I was complimented that Satan considered me important enough to turn his guns on me. I figured if healing really is in the atonement, then medicine perpetuates both the lie and the unbelief. Other mature believers assured me that if I cranked up the courage and the faith to flush my pills down the toilet, I could hold Jesus to His promise to heal me. "Reduce the dosage a little at a time if you want," the pastor counseled me, "but demonstrate your faith by renouncing the devil's lie and affirming your confidence that Jesus is healing you."

I figured if a little faith is good, a lot of faith is better. *Faith* was the issue, and I had plenty and to spare. It's amazing how quickly ego can move in, even on the heels of a genuine spiritual transaction. In my mind's eye I saw myself throwing back my shoulders, pounding my fists on my chest, and crying out to the world, *Do I have faith or what!* No gradual reduction for me; I flushed all my lithium carbonate pills down the toilet and praised God for my healing. I told everyone whose ear I could bend about my deliverance and my super-faith. I was Stan, the faithful witness and anointed soul winner. I wrote to the charismatic *Voice* magazine to tell the editors how great it would be if they carried an article describing my faith deliverance after eight years as a manic-depressive. Of course, the publicity would fill a sizeable ego ticking away inside me.

That is why the editor made the call my mother relayed to me on that dismal winter morning in the psychiatric ward of The City of Faith.

ᕤ   ᕤ   ᕤ

Deliverance from Demons: The Debate Continues

Two areas of long-standing controversy fuel the continuing debate between believers in charismatic camps and those settled into more conventional theological beliefs: What about demons, and what about faith healing? Is it appropriate to apply the label *presumptuous faith* to either of these areas?

The deliverance conflict has been with us for ages, and nothing here is likely to resolve the issue. Still, an objective review of basic Biblical truths and experiential confirmation may prove helpful to both sides.

Bible believers have no grounds for denying the activity of demonic forces. In fact, when we rely upon Scripture for truth about God and His kingdom, consistency and integrity compel us to affirm the existence of a well-populated spirit world. Its inhabitants are active, intelligent, and purposeful, but they are rarely perceived through our five senses. What humans can't see, hear, feel, taste, or smell they are inclined to shrug off and even deny. Yet too many New Testament references testify in specific terms to demonic and angelic activity for us to doubt the existence of "principalities and powers." Much of Jesus' ministry had to do with the rebuking and casting out of demonic spirits. He claimed the authority to call down ten legions of angels in His defense. There is no reason to believe these inhabitants of the spirit world have ceased their activity over the intervening millennia.

God's Whole Counsel

Those who consider the Bible merely a fallible stab at recording man's journey toward maturity may be content to shrug off the notion of a spirit world. Admittedly, spirits are not part of conventional human experience. Bible believers, though, know that when we accept that document as the inspired and inerrant Word of God we must accept all of its propositions. The Bible documents dramatic demonic and angelic activity—both evil and righteous beings in invisible conflict. It confirms the reality of demons just as faithfully as it records the history of redemption and the atoning sacrifice of Jesus Christ.

Consider this for a moment: if there is no spirit world, there can be no *Holy* Spirit. Yet we cannot deny His existence. That would emasculate our doctrines concerning the way the Father provides our new birth, nurtures and teaches us, supplies our spiritual gifts, and employs us as members of Christ's body upon the earth.

They're out there all right, those demons. And for some hapless people they are *in here*. If they are not, the Bible's message is no longer believable. Their ethereal quality works to their distinct advantage. We can rarely detect the demons or angels with our five senses, but both sides are energetically at work. Each does its master's bidding. Tangible proof comes only when we're confronted by some resulting phenomenon or encounter the visible consequences of their work.

The Gerasene Demoniac

Luke 8:26–39 dramatizes some of those consequences in the account of the demon-possessed man who was terrorizing his hometown. He lived like an animal among the tombs in the region of the Gerasenes.

When Jesus appears on the scene the demoniac grovels at His feet, recognizing Him as "the Son of the Most High God." Only Jesus can lay claim to that title. The demoniac begs Him to go away.

The reader soon realizes, however, that this is the voice of the demons, not of the disturbed man. When Jesus asks his name, he, or they, reply "Legion." The reason? "Because many demons had gone into him."

The frightened demons beg Jesus not to order them into the abyss. The King James Version translates that "the deep" and in Revelation 9:1–2, "the bottomless pit." Wherever that abyss is, we don't want to go there any more than the demons did. Luke's account suggests, though, that they knew where they belonged.

Instead of the abyss, the demons ask and receive Jesus' permission to go into a herd of pigs feeding on the hillside. This shows that the devil is not omniscient, because the demons were set up. The pigs rush down the steep bank into the lake and drown. What happens to the demons? We are not privileged to know, but "Legion" is heard from no more. What we do know is that Gerasene locals promptly failed in a test of their values and priorities, a flaw in human reasoning that likely still is with us. Ignoring the former madman, now healed, clothed, and in his right mind, the people see only the drowned pigs and their economic loss. Brusquely, they order Jesus out of their territory.

Here is what Luke's account tells us about "evil" spirits:

- They are real.

- They can overpower and indwell humans.

- They are bad news.

- They recognize Jesus' authority.

- They are deceitful and manipulative.

- They are destructive.

- They know they belong in the pit.

- They fear the devil whom they serve.

- They are not omniscient.

Mustard Seed Faith

Matthew (17:14–20) writes of a man who comes to Jesus on behalf of his son who is suffering frightening seizures. He had brought the boy to Jesus' disciples, but they were not able to heal him. Jesus rebukes a demon, which comes out of the boy. He is healed on the spot.

"Why couldn't we drive it out?" the disciples want to know.

"Because you have so little faith," Jesus answers. Then follows His famous reference to faith's ability to move mountains. Remember, though, that faith is not some physical or mental power generated within us. Our bodies do not possess a gland or our minds a neuron which cranks out faith. Saving faith is God's spiritual gift that comes with His Spirit and develops through the learning process. The gift and the learning process come through hearing and believing, and the hearing and believing are attuned to the Word of God (see Romans 10:17). *Believing,* in the Biblical sense, is best understood as a transitive verb; it requires an object—God and His specific promises.

Spiritual Warfare

H. G. Wells is credited with observing that "civilization is a race between education and catastrophe." In a sense the Christian life is a similar challenge. Conformity to the will of God seems a constant struggle between belief and presumption. We have so much to learn that we're inclined to wonder if the task can be completed in time. More often than we care to admit, the race is forfeited because we lack the time, energy, or concern to pursue the learning.

Many of us concede demons must be real only because the New Testament reports plainly on their activities. A few know about them because they've been personally involved in the spiritual warfare described in the Bible. These few experience demonic activity through one or more of their five senses. They learn to combat those hostile forces through proper use of weapons provided by God for our spiritual arsenal. They know better than to depend upon daring, muscle, wit, or assumption, or to engage in impulsive decisions and guessing games. None of those carnal weapons is suitable in this unearthly warfare.

Enter Presumptuous Faith

Nevertheless, some who profess to know Christ persist in combining Biblical truth with presumptuous human response. Boldness, bravery, recklessness, and enthusiasm dominate their concept of faith. They're forever proving something, as if God doesn't already know. But faith in Christ is not to be confused with mere optimism, courage, or even piousness; it is not an exercise in ego or derring-do. Transactions of faith are not senseless, pointless acts of sacrifice; God prefers obedience (see 1 Samuel 15:22). Biblical faith is believing specific and authentic promises with a specific purpose in view. That kind of faith affirms the purposes of God in harmony with His revealed character.

Biblical faith is believing what is revealed in God's Word and acting upon that conviction, because what is revealed in Scripture is true precisely as God

Himself is true. His integrity is expressed through His Word. He does not treat us as pawns. He doesn't have to test us, for He knows already that we are dust (see Psalms 103:14). Biblical faith is embracing the whole counsel of God as revealed in the Scriptures. The faith that saves us, nurtures us, and makes us useful in God's kingdom is not contained in a simple formula or directed to a single truth; it is the intricate pattern of an awesomely beautiful design—a faith that acts upon the premise that nothing and no one else can be trusted with our eternal destiny.

Those who act presumptuously rather than in Biblical faith may play into the hands of the very demons Scripture warns against. The assigned task of those spirits is the creation of misinformation, doubt, confusion, disappointment, and misguided zeal. Their skills are well developed, but they welcome and can utilize our cooperation. Helped by the natural man within each of us, they perform their task with zeal and effectiveness. To deny the existence or belittle the mission of demons is to make ourselves a stationary target for their flaming darts.

That is why we are instructed to test the spirits. We must take nothing for granted. Though God does not need to test us, He instructs us to test the spirits, for they are masters in the art of deception. John provided helpful guidelines for that testing process when he wrote:

> Dear friends, do not believe every spirit, but test the spirits to see whether they are from God, because many false prophets have gone out into the world. This is how you can recognize the Spirit of God: Every spirit that acknowledges that Jesus Christ has come in the flesh is from God, but every

spirit that does not acknowledge Jesus is not from God. This is the spirit of the antichrist, which you have heard is coming and even now is already in the world.

You, dear children, are from God and have overcome them, because the one who is in you is greater than the one who is in the world. They are from the world and therefore speak from the viewpoint of the world, and the world listens to them. We are from God, and whoever knows God listens to us; but whoever is not from God does not listen to us. This is how we recognize the Spirit of truth and the spirit of falsehood. (1 John 4:1–6)

Does John's formula rule out common sense? Indeed it does not! Even when we test the spirits through the use of John's guidelines, common sense and proper motives are required to read the evidence and check it against the whole counsel of God.

Testing the Spirits

Is our chief end really "to glorify God and enjoy Him forever" (Shorter Catechism)? Then any alternative that entices us with benefits, prosperity, enjoyment, and self-service is not likely to be the Spirit of truth. The spirit of falsehood seeks to exploit God, not glorify and enjoy Him. It prompts us to look always for our own benefit. It makes assumptions. It places *our* will before *His* will. Believing people are in serious jeopardy if they do their reasoning and make their judgments "from the viewpoint of the world."

That warning applies just as surely to faith healing as it does to the testing of spirits. Are we really promised health, well-being, and prosperity as children of God? Our human nature yearns for that, but it is not always what is best for us. Spiritual healing is indeed provided us in Christ's atonement. He died for us in order that we might live in Him. Our ruptured relationship with a holy God is healed through Christ's death as our substitute. That is foundational to our faith. But when Christians ponder whether or not physical healing also is provided in Isaiah 53:5, disagreement arises.

When Peter quotes Isaiah's promise in his letter to dispersed believers across the Middle East, he provides a possible hint as to the correct answer:

> He himself bore our sins in his body on the tree, so that we might die to sins and live for righteousness; by his wounds you have been healed. For you were like sheep going astray, but now you have returned to the Shepherd and Overseer of your souls. (1 Peter 2:24–25)

When he writes of healing, Peter uses the Greek word *therapeuo,* the root from which our English word *therapy* derives. Although the treatment of a spiritual problem is not excluded, *therapy* usually refers to treatment for a physical illness. In spite of that, in the context of Peter's message it seems more likely he is referring to spiritual healing. He does not say, "for you were sick"; he says, "you were like sheep going astray." Not physical, but spiritual healing is the parallel thought. These dispersed and subjugated people needed to be revived and brought back to the fold. Peter does not appear to be preoccupied with their health or prosperity. In fact, he was well aware they lived in manifestly adverse circumstances.

Still, people of genuine faith stand on both sides of the issue. Likely we will not have the answer until

we are ushered into eternity, at which time we suspect it will no longer matter. The Hebrew word for
healed is *rapha,* sometimes translated "repaired." In
various Old Testament contexts it does indeed refer
to physical healing as well as to spiritual healing.
The often-quoted 2 Chronicles 7:14 uses *rapha* to
promise when God's people repent and intercede He
will "heal their land." Presumably that refers to spiritual healing, since the land was not sick. The same
word, however, is used in Deuteronomy 32:39 where
God says, "I have wounded and I have healed." That
one probably fits best in the physical healing column.

Prayers for Healing

If both sides on this issue purify their motives, the
healing doctrine should create no insuperable problems. Those who reject medical treatment and experience what appears to be miraculous healing have no
way of knowing or proving they did not recover by
natural means. For many, the claimed healing proves
only temporary.

Most believers, on whichever side they stand,
pray fervently for the healing of the sick. At even the
most staid, formal, nonpentecostal prayer meeting
the majority of prayer requests are for people with
physical or financial problems: "Remember old Mrs.
Bates who's dying of cancer" or "Be in prayer for Bill
who's lost his job." A few cynics may conclude
prayer doesn't really change anything. Most believers
pray anyway and hope for the best. Whatever the
outcome, they're happy to interpret it in God's favor.

The success ratio of those who humbly ask for
God's intervention but do not press the issue of mi-

raculous healing is probably just as impressive as those who demand healing as the rightful claim of God's children. When analyzing the results, both sides give God every benefit of the doubt. At the slightest improvement their prayer requests are changed to praise. Most of us believe in healing, whether or not we believe in *healers.* But if our theology comes into conflict with realty, we'd best take a second look at our theology. Faith must yield to reality, not *vice versa.* No volume or intensity of believing will change a false premise into a true premise.

The presumptuous aspect of faith healing and prosperity begins when people assume God decrees every believer is entitled to vibrant health, generous income, and stressless circumstances. Does that assumption apply also to humble Christians in cultures less fortunate than ours who are barely keeping body and soul together while living in squalid slums? What about missionaries who turn their backs upon lucrative careers in the homeland to serve Christ on the foreign field? For most of them the prosperity theory would fly in the face of stark reality.

The error is compounded by three additional assumptions not from the pages of the Bible: Answered prayer depends on (1) how genuinely we believe in healing, (2) how little doubt we entertain, and (3) how long or loudly or courageously we pray. In reality, however, the issue is never the genuineness or intensity of our faith; it is always the character and greatness of the God in whom our faith is anchored. The issue is the transcending rightness of His perfect will.

Christian Science: Manslaughter?

Child mortality caused by presumptuous faith continues.

In defense of the Christian Science Church's position on faith healing, Stephen Gottschall, Christian Science editor, historian, and consultant in Boston, seeks to correct what he calls mistaken notions that his church adheres to radical and cultish doctrines. Religious writer Daniel J. Lehman, in a 31 January 1988 article in the *Chicago Sun Times*, quotes Gottschall saying, "Spiritual healing is not a matter of adding faith or the practice of spiritual healing to an existing theological outlook. Rather, it's a matter of the consistent study and practice of a very specific spiritual discipline, which involves not merely physical healing but a very profound change in one's whole view of the meaning of Christianity and its consequences for daily life."

Gottschall defines the somewhat elusive difference between Christian Science beliefs and the doctrines of less formal but more numerous and perhaps more vigorous charismatics and pentecostals. The latter groups teach that God intervenes directly and supernaturally with miraculous healing, usually through the unique power of a healer employing manifested gifts. In contrast, Christian Science teaches that healing is a *way of life* for those who comprehend the doctrines revealed through Mrs. Mary Baker Grover Patterson Eddy, the founder of this denomination. For them healing is nothing more than learning about and acting on God's spiritual laws instead of medicine. Christian Scientists say death and disease simply do not exist. God's spiritual laws, however, can be learned only—or so it would seem—from Mrs. Eddy's allegedly inspired writings, which have only been available since she discovered them in 1866.

Even in Barnstable, Massachusetts, probably few people these days remember Lisa Sheridan. In 1967, though, newspapers were filled with the continuing drama of her story. The little girl was only five years old when she had her first—and, tragically, her last—bout with strep throat. Lisa's mother chose to treat her daughter's disease with prayer rather than penicillin. Pneumonia developed. Three weeks after her first complaint of a scratchy throat, little Lisa was dead. Doctors believe prompt medical treatment would have saved her.

Lisa's case wasn't the first incident of apparently presumptuous faith on the part of Christian Science adherents. However, Lisa's mother may hold the distinction of being the first to face criminal charges because she neglected her child's medical treatment. After a lengthy trial a Barnstable jury found her guilty of involuntary manslaughter and a judge sent her to prison.

At the same time Lisa was losing the battle for life against pneumonia in Massachusetts, seven-year-old Amy Hermanson was dying in Florida from complications brought on by diabetes. Her Christian Science parents turned to prayer instead of insulin, and the child's health gradually deteriorated. In a lengthy and highly publicized trial in Sarasota after Amy's death, the Hermansons were found guilty of third-degree murder and were sentenced to only four-year suspended prison terms and fifteen years' probation. To avoid a possible repetition, Circuit Judge Stephen Dakan also required them to provide proper medical care for their two surviving children. The Hermansons remain staunch Christian Science believers.

Another victim was four-year-old Shauntay Walker who died of acute bacterial meningitis on the seventeenth day of what was assumed to be a lengthy bout with flu. Her mother, Laurie, had kept the child home from the Happy Time Pre-School in Sacramento and summoned a Christian Science practitioner instead of a doctor; medical intervention was not an option. Sadly, the process failed. When Shauntay died, California authorities considered Laurie Walker's action criminal. She also faces charges of manslaughter and child endangerment.

The Case of Robyn Twitchell

Nearly two decades later, on April 4, 1986, a similar tragedy took shape. Robyn Twitchell became feverish and lethargic. David and Ginger Twitchell, concerned for their son, called for help—not a medical professional but a Christian Science practitioner who was part of their church's healing team. The standard fee then was twenty-five dollars per day, usually covered by medical insurance.

Treatment began at once, but was not aimed at the physical cause of the four-year-old's illness. The Twitchells were led in a program of spiritual healing exclusively employing faith and prayer. Their help was to come not from medical science but from a book titled *Science and Health with Key to the Scriptures*. The healing process involved a probing self-examination and the weighing of the reality, sincerity, and intensity of their faith.

This Christian Science couple lived in a Boston suburb not far from the parish founded by Mary Baker Eddy a century ago. Their parents were Christian Scientists, so they were thoroughly grounded in their church's tenets concerning faith healing. Applying that standard, they may have seen Robyn's illness as evidence that their understanding of God or their spiritual commitment was weakening; therefore, they needed to examine themselves.

The remedy for the Twitchells, according to Mrs. Eddy's formula, was relatively simple: they should redouble their efforts at prayer and their study of the founder's inspired writings.

Mrs. Eddy's *Key to the Scriptures* discourages conventional medical treatment because such treatment elevates the body over the spirit. Christian Scientists believe God wants it the other way around. The Twitchells were urged to improve their understanding of Christian Science's basic tenet that sin and sickness *do not really exist*. Neither does death. Mrs. Eddy teaches these evils are merely figments of human imagination and products of an unenlightened mind. Once the Twitchells regained those insights, practitioners were confident Robyn's sickness would be revealed for what it was: something that simply did not exist.

Unfortunately for all concerned, the formula did not work. The prayers of the practitioner went up along with those of the parents, and the probing of their spiritual understanding went deeper. Still, the child got worse. As is recommended by the church in what are termed "serious child cases"—and required, we should note, by Massachusetts law—the practitioner contacted the top spokesman at the Mother Church to ask for advice. The response was reassuring and the therapy continued. Since Robyn was receiving appropriate Christian Science treatment—specifically, "deep Christian prayer"—no more stringent step was deemed necessary.

The outcome suggests that faith was presumptuous.

At approximately ten o'clock on the fourth night after the practitioner began spiritual therapy, Robyn went into convulsions. The frightened parents insisted on calling an ambulance, and the little boy was whisked to the hospital. The records indicate Robyn showed no signs of life en route. At the hospital the emergency room crew administered cardiopulmonary resuscitation for seventeen minutes, but their efforts were unsuccessful. At 11:10 P.M. a physician pronounced the little boy dead.

The cause of Robyn's agony and death was an obstructed bowel.

Pediatricians say in children this type of bowel obstruction can result from a congenital abnormality or from some type of trauma to the stomach area. In a few cases the actual cause remains a mystery. The symptoms include vomiting, lack of bowel function, fever, and a swollen abdomen—not difficult to diagnose. Physicians describe the kind of obstruction Robyn suffered as "unusual, but not rare." If treated promptly and properly, it is seldom life-threatening. Treatment, therapists say, can be simple. In most cases nothing more complicated is required than an enema—scarcely a "medical" procedure. But little Robyn had no voice in the matter; his parents decided for him. Prayer, soul-searching, and faith alone were presumed to be sufficient. Their presumption cost the child his life.

A full two years later, a Massachusetts grand jury indicted the Twitchells on charges of manslaughter. They became one of five Christian Science families at that time under legal challenge in the death of a child.

Parents Charge Church with Negligence

In Bronson, Iowa, Rita and Doug Swan both have Ph.D. degrees. Raised, however, in Christian Science families in rural Kansas, they were, as Rita describes it, "tragically ignorant about the human body." Both had always abided by their church's sanctions against exposing themselves to information about health or medicine. They reasoned the less they knew on that score the better their faith's chances of remaining unsullied. As young people they refused to watch television ads for even the most commonplace health care products.

Looking back, Doug Swan realizes his doubts first arose when his mother died in 1955 of colon cancer after a long and painful illness. In spite of repeated setbacks she stuck with Christian Science and its therapy until relatives insisted she go to a hospital. When she did, her spiritual practitioner refused to pray for her any longer and she was cut off from her church.

In 1970, Rita herself began to experience sharp abdominal pains, which persisted despite the intervention of a Christian Science practitioner. Two years later the symptoms finally disappeared, and the Swans gave full credit to their religion. In 1975, Rita became pregnant with her second child and the pains started again. When Matthew was born, the obstetri-

cian (permitted in Christian Science doctrine) determined an enormous ovarian cyst was causing the
problem and pleaded with the Swans to get medical
help (which is not permitted). They declined, and for
several more months left the matter in the hands of
their church practitioners. Finally, though, the pain became so intense that Doug took Rita to a nearby hospital, where surgery quickly resolved the problem.

When the church learned the details, the Swans
were placed on probation and Rita was forbidden to
continue teaching a Sunday school class.

Not long after that, their fifteen-month-old Matthew came down with a fever. Again, in came a practitioner. "Probably cutting a tooth" was the diagnosis. Fervent prayer went up. A few days later the
fever was gone, so again full credit went to the practitioner and faith healing. But during the next few
months the mysterious fever struck the baby several
times. Aware of the Swans' previous discipline at the
hands of the church, the practitioner saw a direct
connection between the baby's sickness and Rita's
abandoning the faith in seeking surgical help. "Once
one accepts the laws of medical science, those laws
can turn around and strike back in unexpected
ways," the parents were exhorted.

Intimidated, Rita recalls sadly that, without protest, she "submitted to the guilt."

The fever passed, but when Matthew was sixteen
months old an even more violent attack occurred.
Again a practitioner was called in, and again the parents heard a pronouncement that the Swans' doubts
and fears were interfering with efforts to heal the child
by prayer—the problem was the parents' unbelief.

The practitioner stood over the writhing infant and implored Matthew to shake off his illness. "God didn't make disease, disease is just a lie," she chanted. The parents did their best to fight off growing anxiety and replace it with the positive thoughts the church required.

When the fever worsened, the frightened Swans suggested the time may have come to seek medical help. The practitioner warned against any such faith surrender. Medical science, she insisted, could do nothing for Matthew, and if the parents turned once again to doctors it would be "a long, hard road back to Christian Science." They found that especially intimidating, for both testified they could not imagine life without their church. They were caught in a hideous dilemma—genuinely concerned now for their son's life, but fearing if they called in a physician they might learn they had waited too long. They knew their church would reject them for their denial of its key doctrines, leaving them devastated. In the end there would be no help for their son from either source.

Ironically, it happened just that way. After a futile all-night vigil beside Matthew's crib, they took him to a hospital. The disease was quickly diagnosed as a type of bacterial meningitis similar to Shauntay Walker's which, in its early stages, responds well to antibiotics. Now the infection was alarmingly advanced. The physicians would do everything possible, but they could offer little hope.

"Well, could our Christian Science practitioner stay in a room next to Matthew's?" they asked.

Yes, if that's what they wanted, the hospital would allow it.

The practitioner refused to have any part in the compromise. That was the last straw for Doug. "At that moment, with Matthew on his deathbed and her refusing to pray, I left the religion," he says. A few agonizing days later, their child died.

That took place in 1977. In 1980, the aggrieved parents filed suit against their church and the practitioners, charging negligence and misrepresentation. They lost, the court ruling that the church is protected by the First Amendment's guarantee of religious freedom. In 1983, the Swans founded a nonprofit organization called CHILD (Children's Healthcare Is a Legal Duty, Box 2604 Sioux City, IA 51106.) They are lobbying for the removal of exemption clauses in state penal codes that allow parents to withhold medical care from their children because of religious beliefs.

According to the Law

At one time forty-seven of the nation's fifty states had laws protecting the rights of parents, should their faith mandate it, to invoke supernatural healing for their children instead of providing medical care. In a few states religious exemption legislation seems to place both medical and prayer treatment on the same level.

The American Academy of Pediatrics took a public stand against such exemptions in a statement issued last year, and now the laws are being brought under closer scrutiny. Dr. William Weil, former chairman of the Academy's Bioethics Committee, told *Boston Globe* reporters:

People should be guaranteed every religious right possible, but there's no guarantee in the Constitution . . . that you can act in a way that's harmful to others and excuse it due to religious beliefs. And we see case after case, from one end of the country to the other, where children who were denied immunizations and medical care have died.

Religious beliefs, even some considered bizarre, have been granted exemption from society's norms, like refusal to salute the flag and conscientious objection to military service in time of national emergency. In some cases deeply committed parents have refused to enroll their children in public schools. Somehow, though, those exemptions seem to fall into a different category of presumption. Society may be considerably less tolerable when faith is substituted for needed medical treatment, especially for vulnerable children.

Many private health insurance and workmen's compensation plans currently place faith healing in the same category as conventional medical care. Even Medicare now compensates its insured for certain faith-healing costs. Patients who receive prayer treatment from certified Christian Science practitioners or who stay in Christian Science sanitoriums where only spiritual treatment is given are often entitled to financial benefits similar to those enjoyed when people are hospitalized or treated by physicians.

Those laws and policies have been a boon for Christian Scientists and other faith-healing enthusiasts, but one by one the states now are turning from the concept of parents' rights with new concern for *children's* rights. The first challenge to parents' rights in this regard came with a Supreme Court decision in

1944. This was not a faith-healing case, but the ruling denied the apellant parents' claim to religious exemption from child labor laws. The court's broad opinion also included the statement that "The right to practice religion freely does not include the liberty to expose [the child] to ill health or to death." Because of that finding, the 1944 Supreme Court decision is often cited by attorneys and trial judges during faith-healing cases.

Jesse Choper, dean of the University of California's law school at Berkeley, expects all religious exemptions involving medical treatment to be eventually struck down. "Ultimately, you can't say the Constitution gives me immunity because my action is based on a well-founded religious view," he says. Perhaps related somehow to that trend, Christian Science membership currently appears in serious decline. Yet in contrast, other faith-healing sects, primarily the believers termed *charismatics*, are growing.

Though they can produce their own records of apparently *bona fide* cases of faith healing, Mrs. Eddy's followers may soon be among America's endangered religious species. Their theology mixes metaphysics, healing, Scripture, and the authority of the prophetess' mantle still attributed to the legendary Mrs. Eddy. But New Age beliefs now may be encroaching upon Christian Science claims to exclusive metaphysical knowledge, and the charismatics appear to have taken center stage on the healing issue. Curiously, Christian Scientists gain little advantage from the burgeoning interest in faith healing now sparking massive growth in pentecostal communities.

6

ON GUARD
AGAINST PRESUMPTION

S ure enough, the editor of *Voice* told me just what
I didn't want to hear. He liked my manuscript
and the story would appear in an early issue of the
magazine. Soon I'd be sharing with the world my incredible faith deliverance after eight years as a
manic-depressive. The editor was enthusiastic. My
testimony would encourage thousands of doubting
or timid Christians to trust God for the healing He
promises all who truly believe. No more medicine!
What deliverance! What faith!

So I had to level with the man. Sorry about that,
sir. I was hasty—wasn't healed after all. I'm a fake.
Forget the faith deliverance stuff. I'm calling from a
psychiatric ward. The truth is, I'm not healed; I'm
sick, deflated, and discouraged. It looks like I'll be a
manic-depressive the rest of my life!

Why, Lord? If I've ever believed anything, I believed that promise of Isaiah about healing being included in Christ's atonement. I claimed my healing
to the glory of God, not just so I could feel better. I

made my positive confession. I never doubted for a moment my faith had set me free from the agonies of manic-depression. I didn't overlook a single ingredient in the religious recipe. I was armed with all the faith-healing formulas and the vocabulary that goes with them. I used the whole arsenal with plenty of authority—shoes off on holy ground, voice lifted up, adrenalin flowing, Bible in hand with pages open to the specific promises I claimed. My mind was attuned to the powerful affirmation my teachers urged upon me. No negative thoughts were allowed to contaminate my healing process.

In a dramatic ceremony all my own, I rid myself of my lithium pills and flushed them down the toilet. Such crutches were grossly inappropriate for great faith like mine. The formula may have worked for others, but it didn't work for me.

Credit the wise editors of *Voice*, however. My relapse provided them with a new and different challenge. They looked beyond the doctrines and the formulas for healing and deliverance, and addressed reality. They still published my story, but the theme was not faith deliverance. "In His Time, Not Mine" appeared as a story of hope for depressed people cringing under the stigma of their dysfunction. It spoke to the multitudes who seek healing as I did, who in spite of all those Bible promises come away empty-handed. More than that, it was a stern warning against the dangers of mixing faith with presumption.

I told the editor the embarrassing reality and I apologized for running ahead of God by writing prematurely about my imagined faith victory. Thankfully, this insightful man knew of needs among his readers I hadn't thought about. Members of his staff restructured my manuscript to provide encouragement for those whose faith is suppressed, even defeated, by the adverse circumstances of life, who believe as much as anyone else but remain unhealed. The story, as *Voice* published it, shrieks a warning to people inclined to interpret too hastily the meaning of isolated Bible texts. There may be thousands of afflicted people across our nation in the first flush of their newly acquired faith who leap to conclusions based largely upon human reasoning and their desires. Sooner or later, they, or others who depend upon them, suffer the tragic consequences of presumptuous faith.

Some make the mistake of reading their thoughts into Bible texts instead of reading God's thoughts out of them. Others may lack the discipline to search the Scriptures diligently for themselves in search of God's authoritative answers. Many of God's people today, in ignorance, become trusting victims of overzealous teachers. Some of those teachers are not culpable, just sincerely wrong. Others may be intentionally manipulative. We must beware of modern-day versions of the false prophets Moses wrote about:

> You may say to yourselves, "How can we know when a message has not been spoken by the LORD?" If what a prophet proclaims in the name of the LORD does not take place or come true, that is a message the LORD has not spoken. That prophet has spoken presumptuously. Do not be afraid of him. (Deuteronomy 18:21–22)

"In His Time, Not Mine" in the August 1988 issue of *Voice* speaks lovingly to all those gullible enough to believe a doctrine because an assumed authority tells them it's true or because they *want* it to be true. With the help of *Voice* editors my story dramatizes the dangers sincere people of faith can encounter and the hurt we may cause ourselves and others when blind, credulous, misinformed, inadequately taught belief systems prompt us to act impulsively and unwisely, sometimes even irrationally and irresponsibly. The editor's note which precedes my article advises: "Stan dedicates this article to all those who may be grappling with this same issue. He hopes that those reading this story will learn to mix their faith with wisdom when making their decisions on this sensitive issue."

The article relates how nearly nine months after refusing to take my lithium pills and claiming to be healed by faith I began to experience those ominous symptoms again. I couldn't sleep at night. I felt shaky and tired. My mind was racing and I couldn't concentrate. I became reclusive. I went through a period of terrible confusion, receiving conflicting advice from well-meaning Christian friends and mentors. Some pressed hard for me to trust God in spite of those warning signals and stay off the medication. Others suggested I'd be wise to play it safe and return to my lithium carbonate.

Desperately eager to make the right decision, I began to read my Bible to see if something written in God's Word could unsnarl my confusion. I wish I had taken the time earlier. Little by little the answer emerged. I began to realize that my problem had its roots in my pride. I had grasped the importance of believing God, but I was placing all the emphasis on the quantity and quality of *my* faith. I reasoned that the more faith I could muster, the more God would be willing to reward me with miraculous intervention. Yet Jesus said faith the size of a mere mustard seed is enough (see Luke 17:6). The size of my faith didn't matter; I should have focused my thoughts on the size of the God in whom my faith rested. I had viewed my faith as a virtue—a spiritual accomplishment—instead of as a gift of God and a means of His grace. Consequently, I had failed to balance my faith with the wisdom that comes only from God (see James 1:5). I acted presumptuously, and I mixed that presumption with an overdose of ego. In my article, the editors allowed me to give this personal testimony:

> Please don't misunderstand; I am not minimizing faith. I have seen firsthand the miraculous healing touch of our Lord, both in my life and in the lives of others. God had delivered me from prescription drug addiction and cocaine, and healed me of my back injury. In addition, I have seen deaf ears unstopped and blind eyes opened. However, in my prideful desire to escape the stigma of manic-depression, I ran ahead of God.
>
> I had to learn that things will be healed in His time, not mine. Since then, I have learned to balance faith with wisdom, and to accept God's method and timetable for healing. With this understanding, I felt at peace about resuming my medication under a doctor's supervision.

A New Freedom

My story struck a responsive note with hundreds of *Voice* readers around the world. Since the article was published, I've been deluged with more than 650 letters from twenty-two states and seven foreign countries. Most of them testify to the encouragement my painful experiences brought to readers going through similar circumstances. Some of those letters are from sophisticated and highly educated fellow Americans; others are from humble folk in third-world countries, written in English that leaves much to be desired. Some are typewritten, some are in swirling longhand, and some are printed laboriously, as if by a child. Two or three are almost undecipherable. Yet all those letters have in common something immensely important. Because these people read my story in *Voice*, somehow they or their loved ones were brought out of their closet of shame. Letter after letter tells of someone's determination to shrug off the stigma of what an uninformed public still calls "mental illness." Each writer is determined to join the human race again. Many who wrote to me announce themselves ready at last to stop complaining to God about their circumstances and accept their dysfunction as part of His perfect plan. Some for the first time accept the fact that the "thorn in the flesh" which devastates and shames them is physical and chemical, not really mental at all.

For Fran, a Manic-Depressive

I'll not invade their privacy by using real names, but I'll share with you exerpts from some of those letters.

From El Centro, California, Fran wrote to tell me of her eight-year struggle with what she now knows is a chemical imbalance. A librarian with a bachelor's degree in teaching, she first experienced severe emotional symptoms under the stress of an unwanted divorce. As her circumstances worsened, Fran suffered four manic episodes and plunged emotionally into one period where she was so depressed she wasn't willing to leave her bed. Hospitalized during one of her manic episodes, Fran was locked alone in a room. For her safety the only furniture was a rug on the floor. For Fran that was where everything hit rock bottom.

"I am nothing! I am nothing!" she remembers crying out to God. And just as clearly, that still small voice within her seemed to respond, "Yes, you are nothing, but I specialize in making something out of nothing!"

"I thought of creation," Fran wrote, "and realized how much God made out of nothing. That started me on the way up and out of that place." Her letter shared personal comments concerning humbling experiences with the stigma of being mentally ill. But then with a noticeable upsurge of her spirit Fran's letter quoted what has become her favorite Bible text: "The LORD is close to the brokenhearted and saves those who are crushed in spirit. A righteous man may have many troubles, but the LORD delivers him from them all" (Psalms 34:18–19).

I have no doubt Fran will triumph; she is a real survivor.

For Pat in Prison

A twenty-nine-year-old inmate I'll call Pat read my article and wrote a lengthy letter from the Kansas State Penitentiary which he signed "Sincerely Confused!" He was awaiting a ruling on his parole but wasn't sure he wanted parole even if it came through. "I don't have anybody to parole to," he wrote, "not friends, sponsor, or family." Judging by his letter, Pat's needs are gigantic.

He described in considerable detail the way he retaliates when a guard or a fellow prisoner threatens to hurt him. "I tell them, 'Okay, check this out!' and I cut myself a few scratches, eat light bulbs, put my tongue on hot electrical wires, or hit solid steel or concrete walls with my head or fists. Of course, it's only effective after they put me in a strip cell nude."

Is that the voice of a chemical imbalance? Different psychologists or psychiatrists would make different diagnoses of Pat's mental instability, but they would also agree on this basic premise: something is dysfunctional in Pat's brain. Can a man in that condition ever be restored to usefulness in God's kingdom?

There is no guarantee. Neither is there specific teaching in the Word of God assuring us God will restore Pat's prudence and judgment, or free him from his burden of guilt. We are moved with compassion and we'd like to see that miracle happen. We can ask God to do it, and we can state our case for the restoration of Pat's mental health even as Abraham made his case for Sodom (see Genesis 18:23–33). But it seems to me intercessory prayer is *asking*, not demanding or dictating. We can't know the alternatives and we can't know the future. I think we'd better leave the final decision in the Lord's wise and capable hands.

For Doris Dealing with Panic Attacks

From upstate New York Doris wrote about her panic attacks that came without warning. Her doctor prescribed a drug which seemed to help. *How can it be,* she wondered, *that a fairly strong-willed Christian like me should one day fall apart and not be able to cope without my medicine?* Then she went on to lament:

> Keep in mind that as I was going through this ministers on TV were preaching and praying healing. As they prayed, I prayed for deliverence from the medicine and from the attacks. Only you know the devastation I felt when after prayer I was not released from the drug or the attacks. That in itself became depressing. And to make matters worse, well-meaning ministers of the Lord would say if we aren't healed there is something wrong with us. Then they would preach on demonic oppression, so I'd feel more discouragement, thinking *I'll never get out of this because demons are after me and I've been prayed for, so I'm doomed.* Suicide entered my mind.

Does the Bible tell us Christians never "fall apart"? Does it exempt us from the natural consequences if our brains lack the ingredients required to function normally? No, the fact is the bodies of Christians are just as vulnerable to germs, viruses, malignancies, stress, allergies, injuries, organic dysfunction, baldness, tooth decay, and chemical imbalance as those of other people of the world. Doris isn't doomed—far from it! She's simply a child of God who needs to understand more clearly that her heavenly Father accomplishes His purposes in His redeemed even when the going is tough. That specific trust is what we Christians know as *faith*.

❧   ❧   ❧

Elements of Faith

What is faith, anyway? Does it have or even need a definition?

Is there a possibility earnest people who long to exercise genuine faith run the risk of going too far? What happens if we trespass beyond the faith boundaries of what is rational and practical? After all, presumptuous faith may be nothing more than genuine and responsible faith gone too far.

Most of us are acquainted with the havoc a distorted faith can wreak. Yet if, in fear, we shrink from a faith that is presumptuous, will we fall short of faith that is genuine?

Perhaps even more important, how can the average believer know the difference? Can the undistinguished man, woman, boy, or girl in the pews of American churches or on the listening/viewing end of radio and television evangelism be safeguarded against faith that goes too far? Can *any* of us be sure our faith is authentic and mixed properly with wisdom and restraint?

A Good Definition

Such questions become even more difficult when we recognize the abstract nature of faith. Faith is intangible and often misunderstood. Still, that ubiquitous five-letter word is the best available means of describing a unique and highly personal process of the human mind and heart. Faith, as the Bible presents it, identifies those who declare and practice their allegiance to Christ and to the reliability of God's Word. People with faith are those who recognize and respond to His truth—a process that is rare in this world full of doubters. Yet because faith cannot be experienced through our five senses, some find it difficult to define.

One of the Biblical authors, however, apparently found defining faith a simple enough assignment. He managed it in eighteen, mostly one-syllable words: "Now faith is being sure of what we hope for and certain of what we do not see" (Hebrews 11:1).

In the King James Version the passage contains the phrases "substance of things hoped for" and "evidence of things not seen." We are warned that without faith, it is not possible for any of us to please God (v. 6). To paraphrase the rest of that verse, whoever comes to God must believe not only that He exists but also that He does what He says He will do when believing people hold Him to His promise. The Biblical name for that system of belief is *faith*.

The writer of Hebrews does not suggest by what rule of evidence our confidence and certainty are established, but in this landmark chapter he describes in considerable detail the precise actions by which God's men and women of days gone by substantiated their faith. The list of faithful men and women reveals the breadth of human response to specific promises of God. Note, though, the emphasis on specific promises, not on the imagination or speculation of those who believe.

Faith *substantiates* what we are promised in Christ. Operating in response to all that the written Word reveals, it takes the trouble to find out what is and isn't in God's Word. Faith is not permitted to wildly speculate or write its own script. Neither does it retreat when pain or loss threatens. It will not settle for less than what is promised, but neither will it

move presumptuously beyond the boundaries God
has revealed.

In Lieu of Righteousness

"Abraham believed God, and it [his faith] was credited to him as righteousness" (Romans 4:3). Like all
members of the human race, Abraham lacked sufficient righteousness to sustain a personal relationship
with the holy God who had taken control of his life.
In lieu of that righteousness God accepted his faith.
That meant bringing Abraham's values and priorities
into harmony with God's specific promises. "This is
what the ancients were commended for" (11:1), the
writer of Hebrews continues, reminding us of faith's
transcending value in the divine scheme of things.
Faith is presented in Scripture as essential for a personal relationship with God. Believing His specific
promises—not flexing spiritual muscles, running
ahead, or impressing Him with our bravery—is the
dynamic which carries out divine transactions. To
help us absorb that truth, the writer of Hebrews
states: "By faith we understand that the universe was
formed at God's command, so that what is seen was
not made out of what was visible" (vv. 2–3).

Looking discerningly at God's handiwork around
us requires that we utilize a sixth sense called *faith*.
We recognize that everything we see in its natural
state at one time did not exist; it was created. *Created*
is not the same as constructed, assembled, or adapted;
only what is man-made comes into being by such processes. God's part was created, formed from nothing.

Wisdom

How do we affirm that? Science dares not, for it would emasculate its basic presuppositions. Believing people affirm it by faith—faith mixed with wisdom and reason, and armed with facts. The mountains, the oceans, and the firmament have not always been here. Our reason tells us that, for everything, with a single exception, must have a beginning. The single exception is God.

Before the visible things of our universe existed, there was God. Reason verifies that truth if we listen carefully to its voice. If we humble ourselves enough to accept its testimony, wisdom dictates the some-thing-out-of-nothing premise upon which all created things stand. "The universe was formed at God's command." We can accept that only through faith. Faith is the ability to conceptualize and know that God, not some cosmic accident, gave us the universe we experience through our five senses. Thus faith, the intangible, joins with the tangibles to bow before God's creative role.

People Who Believed God's Promises

Faith is acting on the integrity of God's promises. But beware: should the believer not know or understand those promises, or should he fail to interpret them responsibly, the faith he structures on his terms will lack God's integrity. When that misinformed believer acts, he acts presumptuously.

The writer of Hebrews helps us apply the integrity principle to the lives of carefully selected Old Testament characters. He begins with Abel, Adam's second born, whose proof of righteousness was nothing more heroic than the offering of the prescribed blood sacrifice. That proper sacrifice secured for Abel his relationship with God, but it appears to have improved neither his health, his fortune, nor his life expectancy. He died at the hand of his brother, Cain, a man without faith.

Then there is Enoch, the mystery saint of exemplary faith who one day turned up missing because God had called him to Himself. There is no record here of his great acts of courage; we only know that Enoch pleased God. Since it is impossible to please God without faith, we may assume Enoch believed God's promises.

Next comes an account of Noah, who needed no miracle to convince him God meant business concerning the promised flood. Noah saved his family and condemned the world by means of a long and difficult shipbuilding saga. He did what he was told to do. For 120 years he preached judgment to his fellow citizens and built the ark at God's command. Apparently, he and his sons worked without benefit of faith miracles. Noah and his family had to draw the plans, cut the wood, haul it to the building site, cut it to size, peg each board in place, and cover the whole thing with pitch. Then they went out and rounded up the animals. They had to gather food for a lengthy cruise. There seems little that is supernatural in all that.

Abraham was a man of faith too, but that guaranteed the patriarch neither robust health nor a life of comfort. He was a wanderer. Abraham found acceptance with God because he "went out, even though he did not know where he was going." He was ready to sacrifice his son, before God provided a substitute to be placed upon the altar. Sharing Abraham's uncertain destiny was Sarah, who managed to conceive and bear a child in her old age. Jehovah made a specific promise, and Abraham and Sarah found He keeps His word.

Then there were Isaac, Jacob, and Joseph, who in faith had their moments of despair as well as their moments of triumph. Through it all, they believed what God said. They were not always model citizens, but they acted upon their faith.

When Moses pleaded for his people before Pharoah, he established authority by performing miracles. They were not Moses' idea. They were specific miracles, ordered by God for a specific purpose in the working out of His plan and made necessary by the circumstances. By faith—actually, his mother's faith—the baby Moses was hidden for three months in response to Pharoah's plot to destroy Jewish boy babies. He was taken into the king's household by Pharoah's daughter—another consequence of faith. He *left* the king's household when the call came to lead the exodus, and that, too, was done in faith.

Moses gets top billing in the Hebrews review of faith accomplishments. Nowhere, however, is it recorded that he put God on display or publicly demonstrated his powers for his aggrandizement. Neither did he launch out upon some ego-serving campaign to prove God's existence by means of breathtaking miracles. God has no need to prove His existence or flex His muscles. Whether men believe or not, God *is*. He suffers no insecurity in the presence of those who have no faith.

Even Rahab, the harlot, gains a place among the faithful, but not through carefully contrived theatricals. Impulsively, she hid Joshua's two spies among the stalks of flax on her roof and lied to the king of Jericho to save them. She was a harlot who became a believer. The list of the faithful goes on and on: Gideon, Barak, Samson, Jephthah, David, Samuel, and the prophets. Their acts of faith, covering the entire spectrum of human experience, are part of the Old Testament record. They . . .

- conquered kingdoms.
- administered justice.
- gained what was promised.
- shut the mouths of lions.
- quenched the fury of the flames.
- escaped the edge of the sword.
- turned their weaknesses to strengths.
- were powerful in battle.
- routed foreign armies.
- received back their dead.
- were tortured and refused release.
- faced jeers and flogging.
- were chained and put in prison.
- were stoned.
- were sawn in two.
- were put to death by the sword.
- went about in sheepskins and goatskins.
- were destitute, persecuted, and mistreated.

- wandered in deserts, mountains, caves, pits. (see Hebrews 11:33–38)

Some of those distinctions would be unappealing today. Should faith threaten to hurt and deprive, we would cringe from the offer. Yet those were acts of determination, courage, selflessness, and persistence—all done in faith. Curiously, no mention is made of physical healing. And note that the last nine entries speak not of deliverance but of defeat, suffering, and death. The only contribution some of them could make was to die right. There is nothing heroic here—no healing, no publicity, no ego gratification. These heroes of faith were persecuted and rejected because they navigated by the light of hitherto undiscovered stars. They were not performers; in faith that overcame they presented themselves as living sacrifices. It cost them dearly, but they gladly paid the price to serve the living God. In the end, the price they paid proved gain.

Beware the False Prophets

But there is another kind of cost attached to acts of faith, and that cost is tragic loss, not gain. Misplaced presumptuous faith—her mother's error, not her own—will never be more disastrous than it was for little Kimberly McZinc, formerly of the Florida Panhandle town of Pace. In 1988, Kimberly was not quite five years old when she became the innocent victim of a senseless religious liturgy. Sadly, a knowledge of the Bible could easily have prevented it. What killed her, according to a series of stories in the *Jacksonville Times Union*, was not some satanic cult worship, but a purportedly Christian ritual presided over by one who claimed she was a prophetess of God.

The little pig-tailed girl was not the victim of hate or rage or criminal violence. She died through the wrongly directed religious zeal of the intelligent woman who bore her. Kimberly was doomed the moment her mother proclaimed her allegiance to the spurious revelations of one Mary Nicholson, a self-styled spokesperson for God.

Kimberly's unmarried mother, Darlene Jackson, aged thirty-three, was prosecuted in Santa Rosa County for the first-degree murder of her only child. After prosecution and defense alike rested and while the jury deliberated, Darlene pleaded guilty to a lesser charge, murder in the third-degree (without design to kill). Judge George Lowrey sentenced her to seven years in a state penitentiary for the lesser charge.

Darlene Jackson is not a monster, but she had lost touch with reality. She had faith, apparently an over-abundance of it, but her faith was neither based upon Bible knowledge nor mixed with wisdom.

Darlene's defense attorneys presented her as a model single parent, an ex-Sunday school teacher who organized reading programs for inner-city youngsters. She is neither ignorant nor uneducated. A professional public school teacher, Darlene holds a master's degree from the University of South Carolina. The principal of the New York school where she taught before moving to Florida described her as "diligent and rooted in patience and forbearance."

After a brief romance she moved in with an older man named McZinc. When Kimberly was conceived, the couple considered marriage but decided against it. The little girl was given her father's family name.

All went well until Darlene was converted to what was described in her trial as "charismatic fundamentalism." Yet a careful examination of all the facts suggests the doctrines Darlene embraced are far from the foundational truths taught in the Bible.

Influenced by another of her church's adherents to seek spiritual guidance for her efforts at parenting, Darlene began a series of lengthy telephone conversations with a sign-and-wonders evangelist in the Florida Panhandle who had gained a reputation as a prophetess—Mary Nicholson. Mary has the required credentials: speaks in tongues, interprets people's dreams, receives supernatural words of knowledge and wisdom, provides people with messages from God, and sells her prophetic services. The prophetess is also a high school dropout who last worked as a desk clerk in a roadside motel.

Misdirected Faith

Darlene got advice from Mary on disciplining her daughter. Not surprisingly, one of the prophetess's messages from God was that Darlene should begin sending her money right away. Her faith in the prophetess apparently grew as she made regular contributions. As it turned out, that budding faith was pitifully misdirected.

Soon, dependence upon the prophetess became an obsession. Darlene determined she must be nearer the source of the wisdom she was convinced came from God. She packed their belongings and took Kimberly to live in Florida's Panhandle. They shared a mobile home with Mary, her husband, and four children.

Beset by disciplinary problems, Darlene began to perceive Kimberly as a problem child. Soon Mary claimed a bona fide message from God revealing that the child was demon possessed—indwelt by various evil spirits and a wolf.

To have all these unwelcome creatures exorcised, including the wolf, required a process of starvation and physical abuse inflicted upon Kimberly without mercy. As might be expected, this exorcism ritual would utilize the supernatural powers of Mary, the prophetess.

Faithful to her conviction that God was speaking to her through His handmaiden, Darlene kept a diary of the messages relayed to her by Mary. Parts of these oracles were in appropriately Biblical King James English. In September and October the journal shows these entries:

> It [the demon] did not eat Saturday. . . . Didn't feed it because of her behavior. Sunday, it had nothing to eat. Monday and Tuesday, the same. . . . Show no emotion. . . . Let her touch not the other children's toys because she seeks to destroy and kill. . . . Feed her only what I instruct, not a crumb over. . . . Leave the matter in thy servant Mary's hands.

Already, Darlene had parted company with reality.

Under Investigation

Mary's twenty-two-year-old daughter, Tina, panicked when these battle lines were drawn. She reported the child was being abused. A supervisor, Wayne Barnes, investigated the next day but reported he found no cause for further action. Not long after that, Darlene's diary records these November messages she accepted as being from God. They were given, as always through the prophetess:

> Feed her not, for I have no more mercy for this one. . . . she is as a crazed animal. Why do you doubt me? Know that I am the Lord thy God. Obey, obey, I say. . . . Knock her down. . . . Show her the bottom of your foot. . . . Hit her in the mouth . . . spare not the rod of correction . . . speak less and whip more, with severity.

If a spirit did, indeed, communicate through Mary, it was not the Spirit who speaks to us from the pages of the Bible. By this time one familiar with the Scriptures would have recognized that.

In December Tina tried again to put a stop to the frightening things happening in the crowded mobile home. After she called to report the child abuse a second time, a veteran worker checked out her complaint but closed the case as being unfounded. In late January Darlene wrote in her diary the prophetess's latest revelation from God: "Time is at hand concerning thy seed. . . . Her weak state demonstrates my way is the only way. . . . regardless of how thin and weak she becomes, I will sustain her."

Whoever or whatever made that promise soon defaulted. The child was not "sustained"; instead, she was hastened toward her cruel end. Less than a month later, a frightened Darlene summoned Mary in the middle of the night, reporting that Kimberly could not be awakened. The two women tried to give the child warm milk, but she did not respond. With a final word of reassurance and an exhortation to remain unflinching in her faith, the prophetess returned to her own bedroom. Darlene fell asleep with her unconscious daughter cradled in her arms. When she woke the next morning, Kimberly was not breathing. She called an ambulance and rushed the child to the hospital. Kimberly was dead on arrival. The medical examiner's report, admitted later as evidence in the murder trial, reads: "Severe bleeding covered almost the entire back and involved the deep tissues beneath the skin, having the appearance of severe repeated blows to the back, chest, and buttocks."

On Trial for Murder

At Darlene's trial her attorney argued his client had been in "a religious hypnotic trance" under the domination of Mary Nicholson. On that basis Darlene pleaded innocent. By the time the case went to the jury, however, it was obvious her chances of acquittal were slim. Her last-minute guilty plea to a lesser charge likely spared her from conviction on first-degree murder.

From her prison cell, now freed from her obsessive dependence upon her prophetess and burdened by grief and guilt, Darlene recognizes herself as co-victim of the not-so-subtle presumptuous faith which claimed the life of her daughter. She vows to spend the rest of her life "exposing people like Mary Nicholson."

Sadly, for Kimberly, that determination comes too late.

Mary likely will abandon her role of fraudulent prophetess. On February 20, 1990, a Santa Rosa County jury found her guilty of murder in the first degree, recommending punishment by life imprisonment.

Fraudulent Information Sources

Isaiah, himself a certified prophet, used intriguing descriptive language when he warned Israel against fraudulent sources of information about God. "And when they shall say unto you, Seek unto them that have familiar spirits, and unto wizards that peep, and that mutter: should not a people seek unto their God? for the living to the dead?" (Isaiah 8:19, KJV).

Variations upon the theme of wizards, witches, and mediums are well known today. The market for prophetic services is wide and profitable—witness the saleability of predictions by Jeanne Dixon and other self-proclaimed seers. Ancient Roman haruspices foretold the future by examining the entrails of sacrificed animals. Today they're more likely to use tea leaves, tarot cards, ouija boards, and crystal balls. Some seers rely on private messages allegedly direct from God. Often the prophets and prophetesses support their predictions with carefully selected Bible verses, usually quoted sadly out of context. Whatever their paraphernalia, modern prophets tout their ability to know the unknowable and relay to common folk the very thoughts of God. Some of them amass considerable personal fortunes, thanks to the gullibility of people like Darlene whom they've persuaded to launch out on presumptuous faith.

A careful examination of the history and beliefs of America's cults shows most of them linked by a common denominator: a stereotypical leader—someone who assumed the mantle of a prophet and became the recipient of an allegedly special revelation from a higher power.

The only credential offered is the unsupported pretension to a personal conversation with God.

Self-Proclaimed Prophets

Probably there are those skeptics who grimace and shake their heads in unbelief. They consider prophecy yet another claim from the lunatic fringe. But there are others who believe. Our society contains an endless supply of people so eager to exercise their presumptuous faith they'll believe almost anything.

A few self-styled prophets and prophetesses may naively believe themselves to be bona fide possessors of supernatural gifts. Perhaps we should not condemn them, given the human proclivity to wish for power over the unseen.

Of course, a few who claim prophetic office may be victims of mental instability, psychotically obsessed with the idea they are God's special representatives on earth. It could even be a chemical imbalance. They can be forgiven, though tragedy may await those who come under their spell. It is the scheming ones who seem singularly culpable. They are the charlatans who've learned that thousands of frustrated and Biblically untaught people are eager to penetrate the unknown and share in the supernatural powers discovered there. Presumption is a cheap commodity and in plentiful supply. The schemers make their cynical claims to prophetic gifts to exploit that longing for a personal contact with whatever mind or muscle lurks out there beyond reality. The charlatans prey upon spiritually naive and scripturally illiterate victims groping for channels to the spirit world.

When Isaiah wrote of these false prophets, he used a Hebrew word that means literally "knowing ones." By whatever name we identify them, the self-styled prophets consider themselves the spiritually elite. They've uncovered long-hidden information others would love to access. They convince their adherents that they *know*. They claim their contacts on the other side of reality tell them what is going on in the invisible world. After all, who can prove them wrong?

Old Testament Warnings

To learn the consequences of presumptuous faith, ask those who several times in American history sold their worldly goods and donned white robes to be ready for Christ's return. Scurrying to nearby hilltops, they waited vainly on specific dates clandestinely revealed by their prophets. Their futile vigils were held in spite of the fact that Jesus tells us only the Father knows when that epochal event will take place (see Mark 13:32).

Ask the surviving followers of Jim Jones. Ask those in other cult movements who impoverish themselves to give to their prophet's cause, only to find him using those sacrifical gifts to line his pockets. These are people who learn the hard way about presumptuous faith.

"A horrible and shocking thing has happened in the land," the weeping prophet wrote. "The prophets prophesy lies, the priests rule by their own authority, and my people love it this way" (Jeremiah 5:30–31). The inference is that people may prefer lies over truth. Small wonder they are victimized so often by those claiming special revelation. Still, for several milennia we have had God's warning:

> Then the LORD said to me, "The prophets are prophesying lies in my name. I have not sent them or appointed them or spoken to them. They are prophesying to you false visions, divinations, idolatries and the delusions of their own minds." (Jeremiah 14:14)

Isaiah called the victims "rebellious people, deceitful children, children unwilling to listen to the LORD'S instruction." They gave seers open invitation to lie to them about God: "Give us no more visions of what is right! Tell us pleasant things, prophesy illusions" (Isaiah 30:9–10).

Jeremiah turned his attention to the false prophets themselves:

> "Therefore," declares the LORD, "I am against the prophets who steal from one another words supposedly from me." "Yes," declares the LORD, "I am against the prophets who wag their own tongues and yet declare, 'the LORD declares.'" "Indeed, I am against those who prophesy false dreams," declares the LORD. "They tell them and lead my people astray with their reckless lies, yet I did not send or appoint them. They do not benefit these people in the least," declares the LORD." (Jeremiah 23:30–32)

Modern seers still find it easy to "wag their own tongues and yet declare, 'the Lord declares.' " Their prophecies benefit no one; in fact, they often do irreparable harm, as Mary did to Kimberly McZinc. Yet they can always find a following of those eager for a channel to the unknown.

Jesus also Warns

The warnings are not limited to the Old Testament. Jesus also cautions us against the claims of those who think they speak for God: "Watch out for false prophets. They come to you in sheep's clothing, but inwardly they are ferocious wolves" (Matthew 7:15).

On the island of Cyprus Paul encountered a sorcerer named Elymas who claimed to speak for deity. He was an attendant of the proconsul, Sergius Paulus, an intelligent man who wanted to hear Paul's message. The sorcerer tried to refute the apostle's message, whereupon Paul, "filled with the Holy Spirit, looked straight at Elymas and said, 'You are a child of the devil and an enemy of everything that is right! You are full of all kinds of deceit and trickery. Will you never stop perverting the right ways of the Lord?' " (Acts 13:9). How tragic that Darlene Jackson was not familiar enough with "the right ways of the Lord" to make that speech to the false prophetess who led her to kill her child.

Unfortunately, we cannot count on believers being present with Paul's knowledge, courage, and insights when false prophets proclaim their spurious doctrines. Their spreading of presumptuous faith is broad and deadly:

> But there were also false prophets among the people, just as there will be false teachers among you. They will secretly introduce destructive heresies, even denying the sovereign Lord who brought them—bringing swift destruction on themselves. Many will follow their shameful ways and will bring the way of truth into disrepute. In their greed these teachers will exploit you with stories they have made up. (2 Peter 2:1–2)

That is why John exhorts us to "test the spirits to see whether they are from God" (1 John 4:1). Testing the spirits is a good way to avoid the ever-threatening danger of presumptuous faith.

7

THE ROLLER COASTER RIDE

I have a purpose in sharing the lurid details of my personal roller coaster ride—a purpose that deserves priority over sulking in a corner in embarrassment and self-pity.

I became aware of that purpose when I was confronted by a probing question I was afraid to answer. I was completing a legal form before a trial deposition—part of a court procedure which ensnared me during my downhill slide. The question was this: "Have you ever been admitted or committed to a psychiatric hospital?" I was expected to name the place, the reason, and the dates I checked in and out.

How could I answer that? Opposing attorneys would make mincemeat of me in the trial—exposed as a mental patient with a history of flare-ups and hospitalizations. Tearfully, I confessed my failure to my attorney. "I was afraid to tell you," I blurted out, "but I can't hide it any longer. I'm a manic-depressive. I have a mental illness, and I guess that destroys my credibility."

My attorney was unruffled. "Maybe you don't realize, Stan, that manic-depression is a physical, chemical imbalance," he reassured me. "It's no different from diabetes or any other dysfunction treatable with medicines. The other lawyers know that, and your answer won't help their case or hurt ours. Look, you don't have a mental illness, okay?"

I'm sure he didn't know how desperately I needed that. I know now that I'm not alone. That's the reason I am sharing this tale of woe. Thousands across America who suffer from various forms of depression long for a similar reprieve. That door of personal shame, guarded so carefully, shuts out the real world and destroys the vital relationships that make life worth living.

More Letters Come

That must be what the prophet means when he declares "My people are destroyed from lack of knowledge" (Hosea 4:6). Because I didn't know the facts of my dysfunction or understand its implications, I spent many destructive years fearing rejection. I thought becoming a Christian and getting God on my side would change all that, but instead of making things better, in a sense it made them worse. Someone convinced me my faith must be affirmed by claiming deliverance from manic-depression. It never occurred to me as a new believer that God might be using my physical infirmity for His reasons. Perhaps what He purposes to do in and through me is best achieved by way of this nagging reminder of my human frailty. If I can serve God more effectively as a controlled manic-depressive, why should I expect exemption from such personal discipline?

A lady doing contract work for NASA saw my story in *Voice* and wrote to tell me how her second marriage was "on a downhill slope." She knew her uncontrolled mood swings were jeopardizing the relationship and the well-being of her two children, but she was "afraid to seek help for fear of being hospitalized or losing my job." The stigma of mental illness casts its shadow over yet another life. I wrote to the NASA lady, but with all my heart I hope she reads this book.

From Rita: Rescued from a Painful Day

In Charlotte, North Carolina, Rita read the *Voice* article and felt compelled to share with me the way the story changed her life:

> I went to see a psychiatrist today (before reading the article) after much turmoil, to try to determine whether or not the Lord might help me through getting back on medication. I went through almost exactly the struggle you wrote about in regards to confusion, pride, conflicting advice, not wanting the stigma, etc.
>
> It was a very painful day; nothing went as I had hoped. I felt desolate and confused. When I came home, my husband left me a note with your article and said simply, "Read this!" I picked up your article and felt spellbound as I began to read of our similar backgrounds and what you had been through.
>
> Thank you so much for being vulnerable and sharing your story. There are no simple answers to the complex human condition we find ourselves in. Yet today, through you, the Lord showed me He is still with me in the midst of it.

From Sue: Has God Abandoned Us?

Sue wrote from Fort Lauderdale, Florida, seeking help in a situation she described as desperate. Her husband of ten years had abused her, becoming violent, as she put it, "over minute things." His behavior had grown more and more bizarre. He had devastated the inside of their home in fits of anger, terrorized their two children, and struck Sue more than once.

Finally the frantic wife went to court and had her husband committed for psychiatric evaluation. After three weeks in a hospital he was released on heavy medication, but the side effects were difficult to tolerate. He was sullen, had no energy, couldn't sleep, and was often nauseated. Sue's husband endured those debilitating side effects from his lithium (I can testify the medicine does not trigger such reaction for most people for whom it is prescribed) for four years and finally refused to take the pills any longer. When he stopped the dosage things brightened considerably for a while, and the two of them were greatly encouraged. For nearly a full, medicine-free year he did well. Then the earlier symptoms returned, and life for the entire family went rapidly downhill. Sue wrote that his manic episodes were growing worse and worse. Her husband said he would rather die than go back on the medicine.

I can empathize. How many times in my own experience have I complained, "I'd rather die than do that?" But Sue's husband forgot that dying was not a legitimate alternative. The alternative to going back on his medicine was not death; it was suffering those mood swings which, in turn, took such a terrible toll on his wife and family. Not taking his medicine may have seemed a reasonable alternative to him, but for those who loved him it was a ticket back to nightmare city. Strangely, Sue saw their situation as the consequence of God's neglect. She wrote, "When he got sick before, neither of us was serving the Lord. Now we both are, and I just can't believe that He would allow this to happen again."

It seems to me Sue needs to understand that omnipotence is only one of God's attributes. Wisdom and compassion are two others. The circumstances of Sue's life are beyond her control. The only advice worthy of a Biblically-anchored faith is simply "Do your part, then trust and obey." Should Sue blame God? Perhaps Paul the apostle can provide the answer:

> But who are you, O man, to talk back to God? "Shall what is formed say to him who formed it, 'Why did you make me like this?' " Does not the potter have the right to make out of the same lump of clay some pottery for noble purposes and some for common use? (Romans 9:20–21)

God certainly is all-powerful and all-knowing, which means that as the Potter He can do whatever He desires. Yet that doesn't always turn out to be what the clay wants Him to do. There is no doubt He is well able to intervene for any of His children who are ill or hurt. He can heal us instantaneously: Jesus did that often. He can also *prevent* His children from becoming ill or suffering injury, and my guess is He does that more often than we realize. So, clearly, God could make Sue's husband well or He could have kept him from being sick in the first place. But our Father in heaven is also wise and good and loving, and that means we can trust Him always to make the right decision in our best interest and always with eternity's values and priorities in view. We must not forget His perfect plan for each of our lives—a plan that guarantees a better conclusion than anything we could contrive for ourselves.

We seldom welcome adversity, but in God's scheme of things adversity may be a necessary part of the process. He knows what tomorrow will bring—and next month, and next year—and we don't. He knows all the alternatives that are hidden from our view. What seems best to us right now often would prove disastrous in the long run, and vice versa. We will never fully comprehend on this side of eternity how blessed we are that God is in control of every aspect of the believer's destiny. I pray that Sue will come to understand that awesome truth more clearly as she commits herself and her husband to the loving care of an all-wise and all-powerful heavenly Father.

From Ed: It all Began with Pot

Ed, an earnest believer, wrote from Stayton, Oregon, to tell me how a brief college courtship with marijuana may have triggered his manic-depressive symptoms which almost destroyed his life. With a 4.0 average the first semester he was off and running on a great college career, until his discovery of pot. "I started doing bizarre things," he wrote, like stealing paintings from the college's art department and trying to sell them at the student union. He ended up in a psychiatric ward.

Embarrassed by the fact that he was on medication for a mental disease, Ed struggled for years through cycles of getting better, neglecting his medicine, then relapsing, then taking his medicine, getting better, and back through the cycle again. Meanwhile, he married and started a family. "Finally, while sitting in an institution, I was served with divorce papers, and it shattered me," he wrote.

In an effort to get his bearings again, Ed set out to read the Bible from cover to cover. In the process he decided the medicine prescribed for him was God's way of providing healing, so back on the dosages he went, only this time permanently and consistently.

Not all such stories move so quickly from defeat to victory, but the close of Ed's letter gave me special cause for rejoicing. He and his wife have remarried and now lead a happy and stable life. He has earned a college degree in human services and recently passed Oregon's licensing test for insurance salesmen. Ed closed his letter with these words:

> I am well and I handle things now that used to crush me. I have had no problems after being obedient to the Lord. It truly makes no difference to me that I have to take the medication. I have a weakness, but "in my weakness I am made strong."

It sounds to me like a bona fide they-all-lived-happily-ever-after ending.

From Farbie: Learning Through Pain

From Fayetteville, Georgia, Farbie wrote that her mother had suffered profound attacks of anxiety while Farbie was a teenager. The tension caused serious emotional problems for Farbie who, to get away from the circumstances, got married and left home.

When her marriage ended in divorce, she went back under the grim shadow of her mother's depression. For ten years, even under medication, her mother's illness was "hell on the whole family." Then Farbie read the article in *Voice* and wrote:

> Continually, I have prayed for mother's healing with seemingly no answer. But now, after reading your story, I am looking at things differently. In answer to my prayers, God has shown me more of Himself and His work.
>
> We learn through failure and pain things that can be learned no other way. I've learned that problems can be God's ministers to teach, to humble, to focus our attention on Him.
>
> I always felt mother could get off the medication if she just had enough faith. I felt that mother's illness was the consequence of not living the proper Christian life, that it was really her fault. Now I know that God is sovereign and He is using this in her life to create in her the character He desires, for the good of her and others, for His glory.
>
> Mother will be healed; if not in this life, then in the next. Maybe not when I desire it, but it will happen.

From Libby: Recognizing Pride

Writing from Stuart, Florida, Libby pinpointed pride as the cause for her losing struggle with mood swings. A nurse, she had recently been fired after "a seven-month, extremely stressful situation that drove me, my family, and my employer to that crisis point. I was so stubborn I denied the facts everyone was pointing out to me." She wanted me to know that the *Voice* article "probably prevented me from destroying my own life and that of my family." Her letter explained in more detail:

> As an intellectual, charismatic Baptist who's known the Lord a long time and thought I knew everything, I had a real problem with pride. I prayed for wisdom, and as God showed me answers, in my ignorance, I rejected the facts out of pride. I felt, even as a knowledgeable health professional, that taking lithium would be so *humiliating!* I had claimed healing of all of my illnesses in 1987—off all medication for thyroid imbalance, migraine headaches and overweightness.

Seeing the Depth of Human Need

Many other letters reported new insights and encouragement gained from the article in *Voice*. People in many walks of life wrote to report new lessons learned concerning God's sovereignty and our acceptance of the circumstances He ordains. My days also were livened by several pointed letters from unmarried girls suggesting we get to know each other better. Many of the overseas letters were from people who wanted me to send them money or Christian literature, or help them get a visa to come to this country. One brother in Nigeria was starting a new evangelistic organization and wanted me to be the international president, provided I'd enclose a substantial contribution along with my letter of acceptance. A significant percentage of the letters came from prison inmates, some wanting me to intercede for them and help them be set free.

Most of all, these letters taught me the height and breadth of human mind-set and the depth of human need. They gave me a clearer insight into the awesome majesty and grace of God. I am glad I was able to help a few of my fellow pilgrims understand that God will not remain in anyone's theological strait-jacket, no matter how carefully the system is structured. He owes us nothing; it is we who are eternally in His debt. He is Lord, also, of medicines and the medical skills which come as His gift. God heals if and when it pleases Him, but on His terms and in His time and way. His healing methods also include appropriate medical care. Even in circumstances we consider hostile, the God who guides and provides for His own is still loving and kind and always righteous. In His time all that now seems so wrong by our self-serving standards will be made right, never to be questioned again.

Meanwhile, our obligation is clearly to do what we can to help each other.

&a.   &a.   &a.

Help Near at Hand

"You alone can do it, but you can't do it alone," the old bromide reminds us. In the battle to regain control when something's gotten out of hand, those few words capture the essence of what self-help is all about.

People who suffer addiction, mood disorders, physical handicap, seizures, or some similar dysfunctional syndrome doubtless know best the virtue of the "you can't do it alone, but only you can do it" philosophy. They know from experience that help is indeed near at hand. Those who claim that help, however, discover that it often comes at a price. They learn they must accept reality, no matter how painful, and in humility utilize the resources made available to them. Not far behind the afflicted themselves are wives, husbands, parents, children, or others obliged to live with family members struggling against what often seem overwhelming odds. Sufferers and codependents alike can be thankful this cloud of gloom has a silver lining. Whether from the perspective of the victim or the caregiver, those in daily contact with these afflictions find themselves uniquely qualified to help and encourage each other effectively.

Support Groups

Participants in self-help groups usually are generous in expressing enthusiasm about the benefits they are receiving. One comments:

> The main benefit may be the simple discovery that I'm not alone—that other people have similar problems. When someone faces a crisis, and I suppose we're all vulnerable to that, he or she can learn from the others. That way we all help each other until it's our turn to be helped.

Group participants join in the discovery of a heartening paradox. The human frailty which provides the need for help in the first place proves also a source of strength and encouragement. The humbling lessons learned by victims and caregivers alike through the constant stress of their circumstances enable them to better support and strengthen each other. They dare not expect this support to take the place of medical or psychological therapy, but they find it a vitally important adjunct in the healing process. Self-help groups do not claim to offer alternatives to biochemical or psychological therapy, but they can unquestionably add a new and vital dimension to the process of coping and recovering.

Finding union in the very heartaches which bring them together, participants in support groups are able to gather information and receive assistance touching their special areas of need. The common ground upon which they stand gives them acceptance with their peers and teaches them to join forces with others to contend for better research, more supportive legislation where needed, or perhaps more sympathetic interpretation of existing laws. In an increasing number of areas support groups counter the threats of ignorance, stigma, and prejudice through educational campaigns. These are aimed at improving public understanding of serious psychiatric disorders.

National Support Organizations

Today, at least four national support organizations minister to the needs of those touched by some form of mental distress. The oldest of these secular groups is Recovery, Inc., founded in 1939 by Chicago-based psychiatrist, Dr. Abraham Low. Originally it served only formerly hospitalized psychiatric patients. Today, however, more than one thousand Recovery, Inc., chapters around the world serve whoever may need help with emotional problems. Former mental patients lead weekly meetings for each chapter, discussing methods of temper control, behavior modification techniques, and the remolding of cognitive abilities. Diagnosis, medication, and treatment are not discussed at Recovery, Inc., meetings, making the organization unique in that regard. Treating psychiatrists, however, are urged to participate—both as contributors and as learners.

The National Alliance for the Mentally Ill. This alliance was founded in 1979, but already has more than 700 affiliates. The organization has become a powerful force in the legislative halls of Washington and is influential in state governments as well. When congressional hearings are held on the topic of mental health, NAMI representatives usually are called upon to testify. Their affiliates consist mostly of family members of schizophrenic patients, but their programs reach out also to those afflicted with various forms of depression.

NAMI also exerts significant influence in combating stigma for mental patients and educating the public about the needs of the mentally handicapped. In a TV commercial sponsored by the organization, actor Kirk Douglas looks directly at the camera and confides:

> It's been troubling me. Now, why is it that most of us can talk openly about the illnesses of our bodies, but when it comes to our brain and illnesses of the mind we clam up, and because we clam up, people with emotional disorders feel ashamed, stigmatized, and don't seek the help that can make the difference. Let's start now. Talk openly about mental illness. Help us change those attitudes.

NAMI also conducts a "media watch" campaign aimed at identifying influences contributing to the stigma associated with mental problems. When someone writing in the print media or performing for the broadcast media portrays mental illness incorrectly, or makes comments considered insensitive, offensive, or uninformed, the perpetrators are likely to hear from NAMI. Usually a single diplomatically worded letter is all it takes to educate media personnel concerning the error of their ways.

The National Depressive and Manic-Depressive Association. The National Depressive and Manic-Depressive Association is an organization of individuals who have been diagnosed as suffering from mania, depression, or both, plus family members inevitably touched by their plight. Their eighty chapters in cities across our nation sponsor monthly meetings featuring lectures by recognized experts in this field. They also sponsor discussion groups in which affected people can talk about their experiences and concerns and share information about solutions they've discovered. NDMDA supplies reams of informational materials to all who inquire.

Depressives Anonymous. The most recent addition to the list of self-help groups is Depressives Anonymous: Recovery from Depression. Dr. Helen De Rosis developed the self-help method used by this organization. Participants are urged to specify particular problem areas. These can then be broken down into manageable units and overcome through De Rosis' four-step approach.

Expansion of self-help groups serving an increasing number of disorders confirms the fact that enormous remedial power can be generated when the afflicted and their caregivers explore ways they can help each other. This type of support, incidentally, is not limited to those suffering from mental problems. The same growth is evident in other areas of dysfunction.

Anonymous Programs. Probably the oldest and best-known self-help organization—and the pattern for many that have followed—is Alcoholics Anonymous. More recently, Gamblers Anonymous and Narcotics Anonymous began providing similar solutions for those trapped in other prominent areas of addiction. *Anonymous* organizations are available even for overeaters. In addition, there are support groups like Alanon, composed of caregivers and often the primary victims of addicts. All these people with common problems share learning experiences, newly discovered coping skills, practical information, and different forms of therapy and life-styles. These groups create a spirit of community among peers that provides an opportunity to speak openly of experiences, feelings, hopes, disappointments, fears, and even failures in a climate of acceptance where participants can be confident of full understanding and confidentiality.

This kind of emotional support, along with the compassion and acceptance the victims themselves can best give and receive, is rarely available in any setting other than such groups. By working together to tap existing sources of encouragement and help, to stimulate public understanding of their plight, and to advocate improved services and research, victims and caregivers alike are discovering strength in unity and common concerns.

Generating Empathy

And what is found at the heart of this effort in mutual assistance? Simply the profound empathy communicated among people who share the burden of enduring a specific handicap. They've been there and they know. Theories are out; harsh reality is in. That empathy is generated whether the unifying factor is the dysfunctional syndrome itself or the necessity of sharing life with someone who is afflicted.

When Dr. C. Everett Koop was Surgeon General of the United States, he commented at a national workshop on the specific topic of "Self-Help and Public Health": "I believe in self-help as an effective way of dealing with problems, stress, hardship, and pain. . . . Mending people, curing them, is no longer enough. It is only part of the total health care that most people require."

8

EXIT THE HAPPY ENDING

Not all bouts with manic-depression end happily. The outcome may depend upon factors that go beyond man's control. In her book *Wake Me When It's Over* (New York: Random House, 1989), Mary Kay Blakely describes her eldest brother's losing battle with mood swings—a lengthy and agonizing struggle which ended tragically in his self-destruction.

Frank's Story

Frank Blakely enrolled as a Catholic seminarian while still a youth, but gave that up to search for God through the writings of Buddhist monks, Jewish rabbis, Protestant theologians, and Unitarian ministers. Whose representative of God is genuine, and how can we know that for sure? Until a seeker finds authoritatve answers to those questions, some might classify *any* expression of faith as presumptuous.

Frank's sister characterizes him as a profoundly religious person, though there is no indication he found the answers he was seeking. His own thoughts on the subject were refreshingly innovative. After one of his manic episodes he defined his theology by writing, "We are all like bacteria in a banana, each doing our own little thing, while the fruit is ripened for God's digestion."

Early Evaluation of Bipolar Delusions

There is evidence Frank now and then assumed he was God. The delusions that accompany bipolar disorders can produce grandiose feelings of power. For manic-depressives reality often is elusive. Inside Frank's head was a euphoric rhythm he described as "the beat, the beat, the beat." There were not necessarily voices; often it was just "the beat."

Frank suffered his first manic episode in 1967, after which he was wired with electrodes at Loretto Hospital in Chicago and given shock treatments. If those treatments helped, they did so only temporarily. Frank's interpretation of the episode was that he had received messages directly from God. He saw the truth arriving in tremendous jolts, just as he had imagined it would. For this earnest seeker reality was going by the board.

"But truth doesn't fry your brain," his sister pointed out.

"Sometimes it *does*," Frank responded, apparently as surprised to report this revelation as Mary Kay was to receive it.

During the episodes which followed, Frank was tested, probed, drugged, and examined by psychiatrists with unimpeachable credentials, but not as thoroughly as such tests would be conducted today. It was not until later that the possibility of a chemical imbalance was clinically explored. During Frank's early testing periods doctors found no convincing answers to the questions raised by his personal anguish. The patient had testified that his head felt as if it were clasped between the two powerful hands of a spinning discus thrower, orbiting in the first stages of a mighty toss. Much of the time he waited for the final heave, which he hoped would release him at last from the dizzying spins and launch him into free flight. For Frank that release never came.

Typical of those who suffer bipolar affective disorders so severely, Frank emerged from each of his hyperactive swings altered in some way by what he had experienced. The manic bouts were followed by lengthy periods of depression, during which the mystical messages received in the manic phases melted into uncertainty and doubt. Confidence vanished. Everything turned inward. During the depressive phase Frank lived painfully with loneliness. Undecided and afraid, he slept as much as twenty hours at a time. He described those episodes as "grand mal seizures of despair."

Possible Chemical Imbalance

In the spring of 1970, Frank's mother arranged to have him included in a program conducted at the Illinois State Psychiatric Institute by Doctors Herbert Y. Meltzer and Ronald Moline. These two physicians were among the first to explore the possibility that manic-depression is caused by a chemical imbalance. Their early experiments suggested these mood swings are not properly classified as insanity. Instead, they can be the result of faulty genetic wiring—a flaw which could be controlled if the missing chemicals could be determined and supplemented. To these researchers, the cause appeared to be biological, not sociological or psychological. Small, experimental doses of lithium carbonate, however, proved of little effect on Frank.

Since no other medical cure seemed available, Frank's program at ISPI also included weekly agendas of psychotherapy, with family members participating in the therapeutic sessions.

His sister writes:

> I hated the Thursday night sessions when the patients and their families were collectively grilled under the harsh fluorescent lights of the locked ward. Maybe somewhere in the past of these humbled people there were cases of bad mother or absent father or emotional neglect—what family surviving the '50s was exempt?—but I couldn't believe these human errors brought the physical changes in Frank. I knew an unhappy childhood was not the problem. If anything, my parents' unstoppable affection had postponed Frank's crisis. He didn't have his first breakdown under their roof; it happened 240 miles away, at Southern Illinois University the year he left home.

For the most part the therapeutic sessions proved unproductive. Psychotherapy is still a notably inexact science. Some of the sessions, in fact, may have been potentially harmful. Frank's grieving father bore scars from the therapy for a long time afterward. He was catapulted into weeks of self-doubt by a therapist's suggestion that his cold and formal handshakes, offered instead of hugs, had deprived his son of needed affection. That insensitive pronouncement ignored multiplied thousands of fully functional off-spring whose parents also characteristically expressed their affection by means other than hugging.

A Last Good-bye

The weekend before Frank was to take his life he visited Mary Kay to tell her how much he loved her. Not until later did she realize her brother had been saying good-bye. He wasn't depressed during the visit; in fact, he was riding the crest of a manic high, moving about Mary Kay's quiet residential neighborhood with frenetic energy. Late one night Frank stood on the lawn of an elderly widow's home down the street and serenaded her. Voices had told him she was lonely, and he was only trying to share the love he felt she needed.

As his visit drew near an end Frank was unwilling to discuss future plans with his sister, insisting that "it's one of those times when the irrational will become rational."

Frank's suicide two days after returning home was not an act of despair, his sister insists. "In his own mind," she writes, "he was committing an act of ultimate faith. It was a death from exhaustion, from the efforts of thinking and striving, and I was grateful he finally reached the end of his pain."

No, not all bouts with manic-depression end happily, but perhaps it is not appropriate to weep for Frank. He thought of his life as "a divine, inscrutable prayer." As if in a final benediction he declared confidently, "My existence does not end with death."

Though Mary Kay describes herself as an agnostic she accepts his theory of immortality. Who knows? The Frank Blakely story may not be ended after all.

Validity of Faith Healing

Are all petitions for healing in the best interest of those for whom healing is sought? Sometimes God has more merciful plans.

Sheila Walsh, cohostess on CBN's "700 Club" telecast, has interviewed on camera scores of people who testify to God's healing power. Sheila herself believes strongly in the validity of faith healing. However, at the close of her TV interview with Stan Schmidt, where the unusual topic was Stan's *not* being healed, she turned to speak directly to the camera and said with disarming candor:

> I know many of you who are watching have been challenged by what Stan said and don't quite understand [the meaning of presumptuous faith]. Some are grappling with this whole thing.
>
> My problem with our presumption that God will do everything our way, in a way we understand, according to our schedule and timetable, is that somehow we feel God owes us that.
>
> The fruits of the Holy Spirit are borne out of trials, of suffering, of hanging in there against all odds. Fruit takes time to produce on a tree, and so it does in our lives. For me, the real question to ask is "Do you want to be healed, or do you want more of Jesus?"
>
> We cannot run away from the fact that some people have not been physically healed. Does that mean that Jesus is not able to? No. Does it mean they don't have enough faith, or that there is some

secret sin? No, it means that Jesus asks us to walk a road of trust and faith, despite our circumstances, keeping our eyes fixed on Him.

Then Sheila told of the struggle within her family at the time her father suffered a brain hemorrhage. The physical change altered his personality and catapulted his family into a season of tension and heartache. They knew their dad's life was hanging by a thread and that at any time he could suffer another and fatal stroke. Courageously, Sheila shared with an enormous "700 Club" audience the lessons the family learned as their father's condition worsened and prayers went up for his healing:

At times he became violent with my mother and me. One night the hospital told us he would not make it through the night. We telephoned Christians all around the world and we begged God to spare my father. We almost said, "Lord, we're going to twist your arm and make you do it. You've *got* to do this!"

My father didn't die that night. I have to tell you that the six months my dad lived were the worst six months of my life. He was like a tormented animal. There came a time when my mom got down on her knees and said, "Lord, I don't understand all your ways, but I trust you. And if it's what you want, then you take him home." My dad died at midnight that night.

We don't understand everything down here. Why do we think we should? God's Word says "My ways are not your ways; my thoughts are not your thoughts." Trust God. He knows you; He loves you.

Maybe your life makes no sense according to some popular theology you've been taught. The

enemy throws things in our face to stand back and
see how we'll react. He says, "Does she love God
enough to keep on walking? Does she love God
enough to keep on *crawling* if that's all she's got
the energy to do?"

Twisting God's Arm

King David knew something about presumptuous
faith expressed in prayer. In reciting the history of
Israel's willfulness David wrote these woeful words
lamenting the error humans so often are inclined to
make: insisting God do things their way.

> But they soon forgot what he had done
> and did not wait for his counsel.
> In the desert they gave in to their craving;
> in the wasteland they put God to the test.
> So he gave them what they asked for,
> but sent a wasting disease upon them.
> (Psalms 106:13–15)

The King James Version translates that final line,
"but sent leanness into their soul." Translated either
way, David's words dramatize the futility of attempting to impose our will upon God—telling Him what
we want and demanding that He serve it up
promptly, prepared and flavored just the way we
like it.

Hezekiah's Healing

Near the end of his successful reign over the people
of Judah, Hezekiah twisted God's arm and de-
manded a reprieve from his impending death (see 2
Kings 20:1–11). The consequences were grim. The

Old Testament tells us that an angel helped Hezekiah defeat Sennacherib and the Assyrian armies before they launched their attack on Jerusalem (see 2 Kings 19:36–37). Shortly after that, Isaiah was sent to tell the king "Put your house in order, because you are going to die; you will not recover" (20:1).

But Hezekiah wasn't ready to accept that verdict; he was only thirty-nine. Weeping bitterly, he turned his face to the wall and made a case for a reversal of God's decision. He reminded the Lord of his zeal and recited a list of his accomplishments (see 2 Kings 20:3). He begged God to heal him and not let him die. There is no evidence he inquired concerning *God's* will in the matter. He thought he knew what was best.

Before Isaiah got beyond the middle court of the palace, the Lord sent him back to Hezekiah with the requested reprieve: "I have heard your prayer and seen your tears; I will heal you" (20:5). Isaiah prepared a poultice of figs and applied it to Hezekiah's infection; the king recovered. God gave the king an additional fifteen years to live. It was a miraculous answer to prayer. Though the poultice of figs also played a part in halting the spread of the infection, one thing is evident: no healer was involved.

But a disturbing question needs answering. Many believers today probably would do precisely what Hezekiah did. Yet are we guilty of presumption when we petition that *our* will be done? According to the record, the outcome in Hezekiah's case was disastrous. He lived, but under radically altered circumstances. "But Hezekiah's heart was proud and he did not respond to the kindness shown him; therefore the LORD's wrath was on him and on Judah and

Jerusalem" (2 Chronicles 32:25). Pride got in the way. Was it pride that he was the honored recipient of a faith healing? He did not respond to God's kindness—meaning, probably, that the king went on his merry way with business as usual, evidencing little in the way of responsibility or gratitude to the One who permitted his recovery. Presumption often takes for granted what is given by God's grace.

The Consequences

Soon after that reprieve of faith, Hezekiah made the tactical error of showing a delegation from Babylon all of his resources. Because of this blunder—on the surface, a kind and generous act, but one the Lord had not ordered—God warned Hezekiah:

> The time will surely come when everything in your palace, and all that your fathers have stored up until this day, will be carried off to Babylon. Nothing will be left, says the LORD. And some of your descendants, your own flesh and blood, that will be born to you, will be taken away, and they will become eunuchs in the palace of the king of Babylon. (2 Kings 20:17–18)

And it happened just as the prophet said. Before the reprieve Hezekiah did "what was good and right and faithful before the LORD his God" (2 Chronicles 31:20). Then came his presumptuous request to override the already expressed will of God. After Hezekiah's eventual death at age fifty-four, his son, Manasseh, reigned for fifty-five years and "did evil in the eyes of the LORD, following the detestable practices of the nations the LORD had driven out before the Israelites" (2 Kings 21:2). Manasseh also "shed so much innocent blood that he filled Jerusalem from end to end—besides the sin that he had caused Judah to commit, so that they did evil in the eyes of the LORD" (v. 16). And consider this crucially important footnote: according to the genealogical records, Manasseh was not born until *three years after* his father twisted God's arm to win that fifteen-year reprieve.

But that is not all. After Manasseh's long and cruel reign three of the next four kings—all descendants of Hezekiah—"did evil in the sight of the LORD" (see 2 Kings 21:19–20; 22:1–2; 23:31–37). They were responsible for what the Bible calls "much bloodshed." Would Judah have fared better if Hezekiah had died childless at thirty-nine? We cannot be sure of *that* answer until we view the events from the vantage point of eternity. True, the good king, Josiah, was Manasseh's grandson, but suppose Hezekiah had died on the crest of his victory over Sennacherib instead of being allowed an additional fifteen years in answer to his prayer. Is it possible a different kingly line would have turned in a better performance? Our lives, perhaps like the Judeans of Hezekiah's day, are filled with "What ifs?" We insist on having things our way, but we can only guess what the alternatives might be. We theorize; only God knows.

He gave Hezekiah his heart's desire, but He sent leanness to the king's soul. When Hezekiah looked back upon his experience from the vantage point of eternity, perhaps he realized it would have been better to submit in faith to God's better way. Perhaps he understood only then the folly of his request to go on living.

Oral Roberts's Tragic Life

Through the Old Testament record of Hezekiah's life God may also be teaching us that spiritual leaders are as vulnerable and fallible as the rest of us. Under careful scrutiny the lives of those who are our teachers and mentors may not always square with the values and priorities they teach. Should we embrace wholeheartedly a winsome and well-stated message merely because it comes from one recognized for his leadership skills? Things go better when our acceptance depends upon the authority and validity of the message itself.

Few ministers of the gospel generate followings more loyal than those who claim divine gifts of healing or other supernatural powers. Teachers in that particular category are prone to assuring their followers that God will reward their faith with unfailing health and well-being.

Yet examine closely the private lives of heralded personalites identified with miracle-working theology. The traumatic lives of some of America's leading proponents of healing often contradict their own doctrines of prosperity.

Personal Loss

For example, few leaders of high profile have suffered more painful personal losses than the formidable Oral Roberts of Tulsa, Oklahoma. On the bright side, his life has been filled with achievement, recognition, and fulfillment, but the famed faith healer also has known more than his share of agony and defeat. Dr. David Edward Harrell, Jr., his biographer, writes in *Oral Roberts: An American Life,* (Indiana University Press, 1985),

> He is human, earthy, visceral, volcanic. He swings from Himalayan peaks to pitch-black deeps. . . . No one knows better than Oral the human frailties with which he has struggled, and he has confessed to faults profound enough to make him eminently human.

The description, a careful observer will note, suggests the possibility that faith-healer Roberts may also have a bipolar personality.

Only one of Oral and Evelyn's four children has followed in his father's footsteps. Two died untimely and tragic deaths as young adults. The first to go was daughter Rebecca, along with her husband, Marshall Nash, a prominent Tulsa banker. They were killed in 1977 in an airplane crash. Their three orphaned children were taken into Oral and Evelyn's home.

Scandal

After spirited defiance earlier in life—during which time he declined to attend Oral Roberts University, enrolling in the University of Kansas instead—son Richard returned to the fold and became heir-apparent to the Roberts empire. Richard has earned a place of prominence in the ranks of healers, but personal tragedy has plagued him. After a much publicized marital struggle, Richard and his wife, Patti—both heavy-hitters in his father's television outreach—resolved their problems with a divorce. In the Roberts's holiness theology that simply does not happen in the marriages of people filled with the Spirit and anointed to do God's work on earth.

Scarcely had the dust settled from that family scandal when Ronald, who rebelled against his parents and established his own countercultural life-style, was divorced by his wife, allegedly because of his alcohol and drug problems. Prayers for deliverance and the heaviest of parental intimidation failed to get Ronnie back on the straight and narrow; he preferred his own life-style. More unwanted publicity came for the Roberts ministries when the troubled son faced a felony charge for allegedly forging prescriptions at a pharmacy located a few blocks from ORU. Afterward, the struggling Ronnie apparently made a valiant effort to change his ways and redeem himself, but the attempt proved in vain. On June 9, 1982, the world learned that the body of Oral Roberts's son had been found in his automobile, dead from a self-inflicted gunshot wound to the heart.

More Heartache

Even that was not to be the final heartache, however. In 1980 Richard was remarried, this time to a strikingly beautiful ORU student from Florida of Arab descent. Remarriage after divorce is also considered a violation of an important scriptural principle and frowned upon by Holiness people. Again, however, the Roberts ministries weathered the storm. Four years later, a son was born to Richard and Lindsay and was named after his famous grandfather. The arrival of a second Oral Roberts was an answer to the faith healer's prayers and the fulfillment of a long-cherished dream. The family celebrated, but too soon. Less than two days later, the infant died of lung congestion.

In the spiritual arena where we battle life's circumstances, the day-to-day existence of flesh-and-blood believers transcends simplistic theories and even treads occasionally upon cherished ideals. Things do not always go according to our preferences. In the thick of the battle there are surprisingly few formulas for assured victory. Happy endings are not the only option. Wise is the person who discovers at last that his judgment is too fallible to be trusted. We cannot know the end from the beginning as the Lord knows it. Thus our reasonable service in responsible faith is to persevere in trust and obedience, and leave the outcome in God's good hands.

Confidence in God

On earth's vast and cluttered stage the real scenarios of life do not always resolve in happy endings. Supernatural healing has not always proven to be in the best interest of the healed. Adversity has mystical teaching powers. Since no one but God understands the alternatives, it is better to seek His wisdom instead of demanding a demonstration of His power.

We can be confident of only one thing on this earth: the character of God expressed in His wise, unfailing love and mercy. For those who are recipients of God's gift of faith, love and mercy are confirmed in the death and resurrection of Jesus Christ. To those filled with His Spirit, nothing is profane in His creation, including the medicines and medical skills He provides for our well-being.

There is nothing wrong with expecting a miracle—providing, of course, we've determined a miracle is what God wills. The wrongness lies in presuming we know and, therefore, we command.

SUGGESTED RESOURCES ON DEPRESSION

Publications[*]

Andreasen, N. C. *The Broken Brain: The Biological Revolution in Psychiatry.* New York: Harper & Row, 1984.

Baker, Don and Emory Nestor. *Depression: Finding Hope and Meaning in Life's Darkest Shadow.* Portland, OR: Multnomah, 1983.

Braiker, Harriet B., Ph.D. *Getting Up When You're Down.* New York: Putnam and Son, 1988.

Burns, D. D. *Feeling Good: The New Mood Therapy.* New York: Wm. Morrow, 1980.

---

[*] From the authors' perspective and experience the following suggested references have been carefully selected to offer the reader a variety of sources when seeking help for depressive illness. We strongly suggest that if you choose to use any of the sources listed you consult your physician for any advice concerning the material you have read.

DeRosis, Helen, M.D. and Victoria Y. Pelligrino. *The Book of Hope: How Women Can Overcome Depression.* New York: Macmillan, 1976.

Fieve, Ronald R., M.D. *Moodswing.* New York: Bantam, 1975.

Gold, Mark S., M.D. *The Good News About Depression.* New York: Villard, 1987.

Greist, John H., M.D. and James Jefferson, M.D. *Depression and Its Treatment.* Washington, D.C.: American Psychiatric Press, 1984.

Klein, Donald, M.D. and Paul W. Wender, M.D. *Do You Have a Depressive Illness?* New York: New American Library, 1988.

Kline, N. S. *From Sad to Glad.* New York: Ballantine, 1981.

Morrison, J. R. *Your Brother's Keeper: A Guide For Families of the Mentally Ill.* Chicago: Nelson-Hall, 1987.

Papolos, Demitri F., M.D. and Janice Papolos. *Overcoming Depression.* New York: Harper & Row, 1987.

Tsuang, M. T. and R. VanderMey. *Genes and the Mind: The Inheritance of Mental Illness.* New York: Oxford University Press, 1980.

White, John, M.D. *The Masks of Melancholy.* Downers Grove, IL: InterVarsity, 1982.

Winokur, G. *Depression: The Facts.* New York: Oxford University Press, 1981.

Lithium and Manic Depression: A Guide. (Pamphlet) Madison, WI: Lithium Information Center, 1982. Revised 1988.

Carbamazepine and Manic Depression: A Guide. (Pamphlet) Madison, WI: Lithium Information Center, 1987.

Video

Four Lives: Portraits of Manic Depression—Public Broadcasting System (PBS) documentary hosted by Patti Duke. For information concerning this film, contact Fanlight Productions, 47 Halifax Street, Boston, MA 02130. (617) 524-0980.

Agencies for Help And
Information Related to Depression

Christian Medical/Dental Society
(Psychiatry Section)
P. O. Box 830689
Richardson, Texas 75803-0689

Lithium Information Center
Department of Psychiatry
Center for Health Sciences
University of Wisconsin
600 Highland Avenue
Madison, Wisconsin 53792

Minirth-Meier Clinic
2100 North Collins Boulevard
Richardson, Texas 75080

National Alliance for the Mentally Ill (N.A.M.I.)
2101 Wilson Boulevard
Suite 302
Arlington, Virginia 22201

National Foundation for Depressive Illness
P. O. Box 2257
New York, New York 10116
(Toll free depressive illness information line; 1-800-248-4344)

National Institute of Mental Health (N.I.M.H.)
Depression Awareness, Recognition and Treatment (D/ART) Program
5500 Fishers Lane
Rockville, Maryland 20857

National Mental Health Association
1021 Prince Street
Alexandria, Virginia 22314-2971

APPENDIX B

SUGGESTED READINGS ON PRESUMPTUOUS FAITH

Barron, Bruce. *The Health and Wealth Gospel.* Downers Grove, IL: InterVarsity, 1987.

Farah, Charles, Jr., Ph.D. *From the Pinnacle of the Temple: Faith or Presumption?* Plainfield, NJ: Logos International, 1979.

Fee, Gordon D. *The Disease of the Health and Wealth Gospels.* (Pamphlet) Beverly, MA: Frontline, 1985.

McConnell, D. R. *A Different Gospel: A Historical and Biblical Analysis of the Modern Faith Movement.* Peabody, MA: Hendrickson, 1988.

Miller, Elliot. *Healing—Does God Always Heal?* (Pamphlet) San Juan Capistrano, CA: Christian Research Institute, 1979.

Parker, Larry as told to Don Tanner. *We Let Our Son Die.* Eugene, OR: Harvest House, 1980.

Smith, Chuck. *Charisma vs. Charismania.* Eugene, OR: Harvest House, 1983.

Van Gorder, Paul R. *The Bible and Healing.* (Pamphlet) Grand Rapids, MI: Radio Bible Class.

INDEX

A

Abel 149
Abraham 144, 148, 150
addiction 62, 141, 174
American Academy of
    Pediatrics 132

B

Bergmann, David, Kathleen
    and Allyson 46
bipolar dysfunction
disorder 1, 20, 22–23, 27, 67,
    91, 94, 111–112, 182–183,
    193
Blakely, Frank 181–183, 186
Blakely, Mary Kay 181–182,
    184–186
blood transfusion 96–100, 104
Bolea, Frank, M.D. 4, 90–91
Burton, Robert 37

C

Caelius Aurelianus 39
chemical imbalance; dysfunc-
    tion 8, 11, 26, 40, 43, 62, 66,
    142, 144, 160,
    165–166, 182–183

Children's Healthcare Is a
    Legal Duty (CHILD) 132
Choper, Jesse 134
Christian Science 124,
    126–131, 133–134
Churchill, Winston 27
circular reasoning 19, 76
codependents 11, 175
criminal prosecution 16–17,
    20, 45, 125–126, 129, 132,
    154, 158

D

Davis, John 50
de Balzac, Honore 22
demons 14
evil spirits 7, 14, 18, 21, 65,
    76, 111, 113–115, 117–119,
    145, 156
depressed 8, 62, 138
depression 8–9, 11, 21, 25, 28,
    38, 40–42, 44, 66–67, 69, 91
Depressive Anonymous 178
diabetes 8, 46, 57, 62, 91, 125
diabetic 11, 99

E

Eagleton, Thomas 28

Eddy, Mary Baker 124–125,
    127, 134
Elder, Kim 19–20
Enoch 150

F
faith healing 45, 49–50, 113,
    122–123, 132–134, 138, 186,
    192–193
false prophets 46, 139, 155,
    159, 161–163
Fieve, Dr. Ronald R. 27
Foundation for Depression
    and Manic-Depression 27
Freeman, Hobart 45–46, 48,
    50, 54
Full Gospel Business Men's
    Fellowship Int'l. 88–89,
    108–109

G
Gerasene demoniac 115–116
Gottschall, Stephen 124

H
Hall, Gary and Margaret 45
Hallucinations 30, 36
Harvell, Dr. David Edward,
    Jr. 192
Hemingway, Ernest 23
Hermanson, Amy 125
Hezekiah 188–191
Hospital of St. Mary of
    Bethlehem 65
Hyperactive 27

I
Il Penseroso 39
insane asylum 23, 65

J
Jackson, Darlene 154–158, 163
Jehovah's Witness 97–99,
    101–105
Jews for Jesus 85, 87
Johnson, Samuel 43

K
King David 21, 188
King George III 22
King Saul 21
Koop, C. Everett, M.D. 180

L
Lincoln, Abraham 25
*Lithium and Manic-
    Depression: A Guide* 94
lithium carbonate 2, 6–7, 10,
    18, 27, 58–61, 66, 87–88, 91,
    94–95, 111, 113, 138, 140,
    168, 184
Luther, Martin 24

M
Manasseh 190–191
mania 8
manic-depressive (ion) 6, 8,
    10, 17–18, 20–22, 26, 28, 31,
    38, 44, 57, 61, 90–92, 94,
    112, 137–138, 141–142,
    165–166, 170, 183
marijuana (pot) 29–30, 60, 170
Masks of Melancholy 39
McZinc, Kimberly 153–154,
    156–158
melancholia 39, 41
mental illness 8, 23, 28, 40,
    142, 165, 167
Millennial City 19

mood swings 2, 5, 9, 24–25, 31, 37–38, 40, 61, 111, 167–168, 181, 183
Moses 21, 139, 151

N
National Alliance for the Mentally Ill 177–178
National Depressive and Manic-Depressive Association 41, 43, 178
Nicholson, Mary 154–158
Noah 150

O
Overcoming Depression 9

P
Pack, Buford 73–74, 76
Papolos, Demitri I., M.D. 8
Parker, Wesley, Larry and Lucky 11–17
Pelton, Robert W. 72, 83
poison drinking (ers) 70, 72, 74, 77, 80–82
positive confession 17–18, 48, 52, 138
Positive Thinking and Confession 53
presumptuous faith 1, 7, 9–10, 16, 48, 70, 76, 78, 83, 106, 113, 118–119, 123–124, 138–139, 146, 153, 158, 161, 163, 186, 188, 190, 196
prosperity teaching 17–18, 123
psychiatric hospitals; wards 5, 7, 30–31, 33, 85, 113, 170, 182–184

R
Rahab 151
Recovery, Inc. 176–177
Roberts, Oral 192–193
Roosevelt, Theodore 27
Rosenthal, Dr. Elisabeth 98

S
Science and Health with Key to the Scriptures 126–127
Schumann, Robert 22
Sheridan, Lisa 125
shock treatment 65, 182
ships of fools 64
snake handling (ers) 70–72, 77, 80, 82
Spurgeon, Charles Haddon 24–25
suicide 23, 35, 42, 145, 181, 185, 194
support; self-help groups 175–176, 179
Swan, Doug and Rita 129

T
Tertullian, Quintus 100–102
The Anatomy of Melancholy 38
The Persecuted Prophets 72
Twitchell, Robyn, David and Ginger 126–128

U
unipolar disorder 20, 67

V
Voice magazine 6, 85, 137–139, 141, 167, 172–173

W
Wake Me When It's Over 181
Walker, Shauntay 126
Walsh, Sheila 186–188
Watchtower Society 96,
    98–100, 102–105

We Let Our Son Die 11
White, John 39
Williams, Jimmy Ray 70–71,
    73–75
Williams, Richard Lee 82–83

ABOUT THE AUTHORS

Tom Watson, Jr. is a Presbyterian minister, family counselor, and former TEAM missionary to Japan and Korea, who resides in Miami Shores, Florida. This is his eighth book. His wife, Diane, is a business administrator for a Miami residential ministry for work release felons. Tom leads writing workshops throughout Florida for aspiring inspirational writers, and his articles appear frequently in Christian periodicals.

Stan Schmidt, a Jewish Christian, was a diagnosed manic-depressive when he was introduced to the Messiah by charismatic believers. This book chronicles his experiences in the exercise of presumptuous faith concerning the chemical imbalance responsible for his mood swings when he was persuaded to stop taking his medication. A licensed private investigator, living in Hallandale, Florida, he also travels widely in an evangelistic ministry and is a frequent guest on radio and television talk shows.

The typeface for the text of this book is *Palatino*. This type—best known as a contemporary *italic* typeface—was a post-World War II design crafted by the talented young German calligrapher Hermann Zapf. For inspiration, Zapf drew upon the writing legacy of a group of Italian Renaissance writing masters, in which the typeface's namesake, Giovanni Battista Palatino, was numbered. Giovanni Palatino's *Libro nuovo d'imparare a scrivera* was published in Rome in 1540 and became one of the most used, wide-ranging writing manuals of the sixteenth century. Zapf was an apt student of the European masters, and contemporary *Palatino* is one of his contributions to modern typography.

Substantive Editing:
Michael S. Hyatt

Copy Editing:
Susan Kirby

Cover Design:
Steve Diggs & Friends
Nashville, Tennessee

Page Composition:
Xerox Ventura Publisher
Printware 720 IQ Laser Printer

Printing and Binding:
Maple-Vail Book Group
York, Pennsylvania

Cover Printing:
Strine Printing
York, Pennsylvania